ESTATE PUBLICATIONS

DORSET

Street Maps of 51 Towns
with index
Road Map with index
Population Gazetteer
Administrative Districts

Street plans prepared and published by ESTATE PUBLICATIONS and based upon the ORDNANCE SURVEY maps with the sanction of the controller of H.M. Stationery office.   Crown copyright reserved

Tne publishers acknowledge the co-operation of the local authorities of towns represented in this atlas and Dorset County Council.

ISBN 086084 322X

ESTATE PUBLICATIONS

STREET ATLASES

ASHFORD, TENTERDEN
BASILDON, BRENTWOOD
BASINGSTOKE, ANDOVER
BOURNEMOUTH, POOLE, CHRISTCHURCH
BRIGHTON, LEWES, NEWHAVEN, SEAFORD
BROMLEY, (London Borough)
CHELMSFORD, BRAINTREE, MALDON, WITHAM
CHICHESTER, BOGNOR REGIS
COLCHESTER, CLACTON
CRAWLEY & MID SUSSEX
DERBY, HEANOR, CASTLE DONINGTON
EDINBURGH
FAREHAM, GOSPORT
FOLKESTONE, DOVER, DEAL
GLOUCESTER, CHELTENHAM
GRAVESEND, DARTFORD
GUILDFORD, WOKING
HASTINGS, EASTBOURNE, HAILSHAM
HIGH WYCOMBE
I. OF WIGHT TOWNS
LEICESTER
MAIDSTONE
MEDWAY, GILLINGHAM
NOTTINGHAM, EASTWOOD, HUCKNALL, ILKESTON
PLYMOUTH, IVYBRIDGE, SALTASH, TORPOINT
PORTSMOUTH, HAVANT
READING
REIGATE, BANSTEAD, REDHILL
RYE & ROMNEY MARSH
ST. ALBANS, WELWYN, HATFIELD
SALISBURY, AMESBURY, WILTON
SEVENOAKS
SHREWSBURY
SLOUGH, MAIDENHEAD
SOUTHAMPTON, EASTLEIGH
SOUTHEND-ON-SEA
SWALE (Sittingbourne, Faversham, I. of Sheppey)
SWINDON
TELFORD
THANET, CANTERBURY, HERNE BAY, WHITSTABLE
TORBAY
TUNBRIDGE WELLS, TONBRIDGE, CROWBOROUGH
WINCHESTER, NEW ALRESFORD
WORTHING, LITTLEHAMPTON, ARUNDEL

COUNTY ATLASES

AVON & SOMERSET
BERKSHIRE
CHESHIRE
CORNWALL
DEVON
DORSET
ESSEX
HAMPSHIRE
HERTFORDSHIRE
KENT (64pp)
KENT (128pp)
SHROPSHIRE
SURREY
SUSSEX (64pp)
SUSSEX (128pp)
WILTSHIRE

LEISURE MAPS

SOUTH EAST (1:200,000)
KENT & EAST SUSSEX (1:150,000)
SURREY & SUSSEX (1:150,000)
SOUTHERN ENGLAND (1:200,000)
ISLE OF WIGHT (1:50,000)
WESSEX (1:200,000)
DEVON & CORNWALL (1:200,000)
CORNWALL (1:180,000)
DEVON (1:200,000)
DARTMOOR & SOUTH DEVON COAST (1:100,000)
GREATER LONDON (1:80,000)
EAST ANGLIA (1:250,000)
THAMES & CHILTERNS (1:200,000)
COTSWOLDS & WYEDEAN (1:200,000)
HEART OF ENGLAND (1:250,000)
WALES (1:250,000)
THE SHIRES OF MIDDLE ENGLAND (1:250,000)
SHROPSHIRE, STAFFORDSHIRE (1:200,000)
SNOWDONIA (1:125,000)
YORKSHIRE & HUMBERSIDE (1:250,000)
YORKSHIRE DALES (1:125,000)
NORTH YORK MOORS (1:125,000)
NORTH WEST ENGLAND (1:200,000)
ISLE OF MAN (1:60,000)
NORTH PENNINES & LAKES (1:200,000)
LAKE DISTRICT (1:75,000)
BORDERS OF ENGLAND & SCOTLAND (1:200,000)
BURNS COUNTRY (1:200,000)
HEART OF SCOTLAND (1:200,000)
LOCH LOMOND & TROSSACHS (1:150,000)
PERTHSHIRE (1:150,000)
FORT WILLIAM, BEN NEVIS, GLEN COE (1:185,000)
IONA (1:10,000) & MULL (1:115,000)
GRAMPIAN HIGHLANDS (1:185,000)
LOCH NESS & INVERNESS (1:150,000)
AVIEMORE & SPEY VALLEY (1:150,000)
SKYE & LOCHALSH (1:130,000)
CAITHNESS & SUTHERLAND (1:185,000)
OUTER HEBRIDES (1:125,000)
ORKNEY & SHETLAND (1,128,000)
SCOTLAND (1:500,000)
GREAT BRITAIN (1:1,100,000)

ROAD ATLAS

MOTORING IN THE SOUTH (1:200,000)

EUROPEAN LEISURE MAPS

EUROPE (1:3,100,00)
BENELUX (1:600,000)
FRANCE (1:1,000,000)
GERMANY (1:1,000,000)
GREECE & THE AEGEAN (1:1,000,000)
IRELAND (1:625,000)
ITALY (1:1,000,000)
MEDITERRANEAN CRUISING (1:5,000,000)
SCANDINAVIA (1:2,600,000)
SPAIN & PORTUGAL (1:1,000,000)
THE ALPS (1:1,000,000)

ESTATE PUBLICATIONS are also
sole distributors in the U.K. for:
ORDNANCE SURVEY, Republic of Ireland
ORDNANCE SURVEY, Northern Ireland

Catalogue and prices from ESTATE PUBLICATIONS,
Bridewell House, Tenterden, Kent TN30 6JB.

CONTENTS

DORSET ADMINISTRATIVE DISTRICTS: pages 4—5

DORSET ROAD MAP Scale: 3 miles to 1 inch   pages 8—13

GAZETTEER INDEX TO ROAD MAP: pages 6—7
(with populations)

TOWN CENTRE STREET MAPS:

Alderholt	page 14	Lychett Matravers	page 34
Beaminster	14	Lychett Minster	35
Bere Regis	15	Maiden Newton	35
Blandford Camp	16	Melcombe Regis	
Blandford Forum	17	(Weymouth)	49
Boscombe	19	Mudeford (Christchurch)	27
Bothenhampton	21	Pimperne	16
Bournemouth	18	Poole	36
Bovington Camp	22	Preston	37
Bridport	20	Puddletown	37
Broadmayne	15	Radipole (Weymouth)	48
Broadwey	47	Shaftesbury	38
Burton Bradstock	22	Sherborne	39
Charminster	23	Shillingstone	40
Charmouth	23	Stalbridge	41
Chickerell	24	Sturminster Newton	41
Child Okeford	40	Swanage	43
Christchurch	26	Upwey	47
Corfe Castle	24	Verwood	44
Corfe Mullen	25	Wareham	45
Crossweys	46	West Bay (Bridport)	21
Dorchester	28-29	West Knighton	15
Easton	31	West Lulworth	46
Fortuneswell		West Moors	52
(Isle of Portland)	30	Weymouth	51
Gillingham	32	Wimborne Minster	53
Langton Matravers	42	Wool	54
Lyme Regis	33	Wyke Regis (Weymouth)	50

INDEX TO STREETS   pages 54-64

One-way street	→	Post Office	●
Pedestrian Precinct	▨	Public Convenience	©
Car Park	Ⓟ	Place of worship	✛

3

Chedzoy
Sutton Mallet
Moorlinch
Ashcott
West Bradley
East Pennard
Pylle
Ditcheat
Milton Clevedon
Bruton Forest
Brewham
Kilmington

Greinton
Pedwell
Walton
Street
Parbrook
Wraxall
Lamyatt
Hardway

Westonzoyland
Butleigh Wootton
Alhampton
Bruton

King's Sedge Moor
Ham Street
Baltonsborough
Hornblotton Green
Redlynch

Middlezoy
Henley
Butleigh
Southwood
Pitcombe
Cole
Barrow

Dundon
Compton Dundon
Barton St. David
Lydford
Alford
Lovington
Castle Cary
Shepton Montague

Othery
Littleton
Kingweston
Galhampton
Charlton Musgrove

Burrow Bridge
High Ham
Keinton Mandeville
Babcary
Bratton Seymour
Leigh Common

Lyng
Aller
Low Ham
Somerton
South Burrow
North Barrow
Yarlington
Wincanton
Stoke Trister
Cucklington

Athelney
Stathe
Pitney
Charlton Mackrell
Charlton Adam
Nth. Cadbury
Holton
Lattiford

Stoke St. Gregory
Langport
Kingsdon
Sparkford
Compton Pauncefoot
Cheriton
Buckhorn Weston

Curry Rivel
Huish Episcopi
Drayton
Muchelney
Long Sutton
Podimore
Sth. Cadbury
Horsington
Kington Magna

Fivehead
Long Load
Ilchester
Yeovilton
West Camel
Queen Camel
Sutton Montis
Charlton Horethorne
Stowell
Abbas Combe
Templecombe

Curry Mallet
Isle Brewers
Hambridge
Kingsbury Episcopi
Stapleton
Limington
Chilton Cantelo
Marston Magna
Corton Denham
Milborne Wick
Yenston
Fifehead Magdalen

Isle Abbotts
Westport
Ash
Tintinhull
Rimpton
Sandford Orcas
Milborne Port
Henstridge
Henstridge Marsh

Barrington
East Lambrook
Martock
Chilthorne Domer
Yeovil Marsh
Mudford
Adber
Poyntington
Oborne
Marnhull

Ilton
Puckington
South Petherton
Stoke sub Hamdon
Trent
Nether Compton
Goathill
Purse Caundle
Stalbridge

Shepton Beauchamp
Seavington St. Michael
Norton sub Hamdon
Montacute
YEOVIL
Sherborne
Stalbridge Weston

Ilminster
Seavington St. Mary
Lopen
Chiselborough
Odcombe
Barwick
Bradford Abbas
Nth. Wootton
Allweston
Bishop's Caundle
Sturminster Newton

Kingstone
Dinnington
Merriott
West Chinnock
West Coker
N. Coker
Stoford
Lillington
Folke
Lydlinch

Dowlish Wake
Hinton St. George
East Chinnock
East Coker
Thornford
Longburton
Fifehead Neville

Cudworth
Chillington
Haselbury Plucknett
Hardington Mandeville
Ryme Intrinseca
Beer Hackett
Crouch Hill
King's Stag

Chaffcombe
Crewkerne
Nth. Perrott
Hardington Marsh
Yetminster
Holnest

Cricket St. Thomas
Hewish
Misterton
Halstock
Melbury Osmond
Leigh
Glanvilles Wootton
Hazelbury Bryan
Kingston

Forton
Wayford
Winsham
Clapton
Sth. Perrott
Corscombe
Chetnole
Hermitage
Middlemarsh
Woolland

Seaborough
Mosterton
Chedington
West Chelborough
Evershot
Melbury Sampford
Melbury Bubb
Lyon's Gate
Duntish
Mappowder
High Ans...

Drimpton
Holywell
Minterne Magna
Buckland Newton

Thorncombe
Burstock
Broadwindsor
Rampisham
Frome St. Quintin
Batcombe
Up Cerne
Alton Pancras
Plush
Melcombe Bingham

Hawkchurch
Stoke Abbott
Beaminster
West Dorset
Up Sydling
Cerne Abbas
Bingham's Melcombe

Bettiscombe
Netherbury
Hooke
Cattistock
Sydling St. Nicholas
Piddletrenthide

Marshwood
Pilsdon
Mapperton
North Poorton
Chilfrome
Nether Cerne
White Lackington

Salwayash
Melplash
Toller Porcorum
Maiden Newton
Godmanstone
Piddlehinton

Wootton Fitzpaine
Whitchurch Canonicorum
Broadoak
Powerstock
Toller Fratrum
Wynford Eagle
Forston

Ryall
Nettlecombe
West Compton
Frampton
Grimstone
Stratton
Puddletown

Charmouth
Morcombelake
Bradpole
Loders
Compton Valence
Peverell Bradford
Charminster

Symondsbury
Bridport
Askerswell
Kingston Russell
DORCHESTER
Stinsford
West Stafford
Tincleton

Uplyme
Chideock
Walditch
Shipton Gorge
Chilcombe
Long Bredy
Winterbourne Abbas
Winterbourne Steepleton
Martinstown
Woodsf...

Lyme Regis
Eype
Bothenhampton
Litton Cheney
Punknowle
Littlebredy
West Knighton

West Bay
Burton Bradstock
Swyre
West Bexington
Abbotsbury
Portesham
Winterborne Monkton
Winterborne Herringston
Broadmayne
Warmwell

WEYMOUTH

Weymouth and Portland

Wyke Regis

Fortuneswell

Weston

Bill of Portland

Grove

Easton

Southwell

ISLE OF PORTLAND

Rodden
Upwey
Broadwey
Bincombe
Preston
Osmington
Owermoigne
Poxwell

Langton Herring
Chickerell
Melcombe Regis
Osmington Mills
Holworth

Weymouth and Portland
WEYMOUTH

Chesil Beach
Chaldon...
Wyke Regis

Blackmoor Vale

GAZETTEER INDEX TO ROAD MAP
With populations

County of Dorset population **595,415**

Districts:
Bournemouth **145,704**
Christchurch **37,986**
North Dorset **46,774**
Poole **119,316**
Purbeck **40,778**
West Dorset **78,849**
Weymouth and Portland **57,547**
Wimborne **68,461**

Abbotsbury **393**	11 C3
Adber	8 A2
Affpuddle **429**	12 A2
Alderholt **1,688**	9 D2
Allington **437**	*
Allweston	8 A2
Almer	12 B2
Alton Pancras **114**	11 D1
Anderson **53**	12 A1
Arne **1,046**	12 B3
Ashley Heath	13 C1
Ashmore **165**	9 C2
Askerswell **147**	10 B2
Athelhampton **36**	*
Batcombe **103**	11 C1
Beaminster **2,380**	10 B1
Bearwood	13 C2
Beer Hacket **89**	8 A2
Bere Regis **1,449**	12 A2
Bettiscombe **93**	10 A2
Bincombe **95**	11 D3
Bingham's Melcombe	12 A2
Bishop's Caundle **349**	8 A2
Blandford Forum,	
E.C. Wed **3,957**	12 A1
Blandford St Mary **447**	12 B1
Bloxworth **196**	12 A2
Boscombe	13 C2
Bothenhampton **1,694**	10 B2
Bournemouth,	
E.C. Wed **145,704**	13 C2
Bourton **670**	8 B1
Bovington	12 A2
Bradford Abbas **960**	8 A2
Bradford Peverell **349**	11 C2
Bradpole **1,624**	10 B2
Branksome	13 C2
Briantspuddle	12 A2
Bridport, E.C. Thurs **6,921**	10 B2
Broadmayne **877**	11 D3
Broadoak	10 B2
Broadstone	12 B2
Broadwey	11 C3
Broadwindsor **1,124**	10 B1
Broom Hill	13 C1
Bryanston **386**	12 A1
Buckhorn Weston **315**	8 B1
Buckland Newton **493**	11 D1
Burleston **36**	12 A2
Burstock **119**	10 B1
Burton **4,044**	13 D2
Burton Bradstock **768**	10 B2
Canford Bottom	13 C2
Cann **692**	9 C1
Cann Common	9 C1
Cashmoor	9 C2
Castleton **154**	*
Catherston Leweston **63**	*
Cattistock **481**	11 C2
Caundle Marsh **53**	*

Cerne Abbas **573**	11 C1
Chalbury Common **145**	13 C1
Chaldon Herring or	
E. Chaldon **130**	12 A3
Charlestown	11 C3
Charlton Marshall **702**	12 B1
Charminster **2,084**	11 D2
Charmouth **1,121**	10 A2
Chedington **96**	10 B1
Cheselbourne **252**	12 A2
Chetnole **305**	11 C1
Chettle **75**	9 C2
Chickerell **3,660**	11 C3
Chideock **648**	10 B2
Chilcombe **14**	10 B2
Child Okeford **942**	8 B2
Chilfrome **42**	11 C2
Christchurch,	
E.C. Wed **33,942**	13 D2
Church Knowle **337**	12 B3
Clapgate	12 B1
Clifton Maybank **57**	*
Colehill, E.C. Thurs **6,728**	12 B2
Compton Abbas **227**	8 B2
Compton Valence **38**	11 C2
Coombe Keynes **89**	12 A3
Corfe Castle **1,338**	12 B3
Corfe Mullen **8,399**	12 B2
Corscombe **355**	10 B1
Cranborne **596**	9 D2
Crouch Hill	8 A2
Deanland	9 C2
Dewlish **251**	12 A2
Dorchester,	
E.C. Thurs **14,225**	11 C2
Drimpton	10 B1
Duntish	11 D1
Durweston **304**	8 B2
East Burton	12 A3
E. Chelborough **55**	*
East Creech	12 B3
East End	12 B2
East Holme **70**	*
East Knighton	12 A3
East Lulworth **218**	12 A3
East Morden	12 B2
Easton, E.C. Wed (with	
Fortuneswell **12,405**)	10 A3
East Stoke **464**	12 A3
East Stour **467**	8 B1
Edmondsham **138**	9 D2
Ensbury	13 C2
Evershot **224**	11 C1
Eype	10 B2
Farnham **176**	9 C2
Ferndown, E.C. Wed (with	
Hampreston **15,549**)	13 C2
Fifehead Magdalen **93**	8 B2
Fifehead Neville **159**	8 B2
Fleet **97**	*
Folke **350**	8 A2
Fontmell Magna **565**	9 C2
Forston	11 C2
Fortuneswell (with	
Easton **12,405**)	10 A3
Frampton **389**	11 C2
Frome St Quintin **133**	11 C1
Frome Vauchurch **132**	*
Gaunt's Common	12 B1

Gillingham, E.C. Thurs **5,449**	8 B1
Glanvilles Wootton **206**	11 D1
Goathill **23**	8 A2
Godmanstone **117**	11 C2
Grimstone	11 C2
Grove	10 A3
Gussage All Saints **204**	9 C2
Gussage St Michael **212**	9 C2
Guy's Marsh	8 B2
Halstock **354**	10 B1
Hammoon **37**	8 B2
Hampreston, E.C. Wed	
(with Ferndown **15,549**)	13 C2
Hamworthy	12 B2
Hanford **31**	*
Harman's Cross	12 B3
Haydon **41**	*
Hazelbury Brian **582**	8 B2
Hermitage **94**	11 C1
Highcliffe	13 D2
Higher Ansty	12 A1
Hilfield **79**	*
Hilton **396**	12 A1
Hinton Martell **293**	12 B1
Hinton Parva **64**	*
Hinton St Mary **181**	8 B2
Holnest **191**	8 A2
Holt **1,194**	13 C1
Holton Heath	12 B2
Holworth	12 A3
Holywell **393**	11 C1
Hooke **96**	10 B2
Horton **500**	13 C1
Hurn **413**	13 C2
Ibberton **107**	12 A1
Iwerne Courtney	
or Shroton **419**	9 C2
Iwerne Minster **651**	8 B2
Iwern Stepleton **25**	*
Kimmeridge **75**	12 B3
King's Stag	8 B2
Kingston	8 B2
Kingston (Purbeck)	12 B3
Kingston Russell **52**	11 C2
Kington Magna **341**	8 B1
Knap Corner	8 B1
Langton Herring **140**	11 C3
Langton Long Blandford **531**	*
Langton Matravers **898**	12 B3
Leigh **390**	8 A2
Leweston **32**	*
Lillington **88**	8 A2
Littlebredy **80**	11 C3
Litton Cheney **269**	10 B2
Loders **502**	10 B2
Long Bredy **184**	11 C2
Longburton **420**	8 A2
Long Crichel **87**	9 C2
Longham	13 C2
Lydlinch **364**	8 B2
Lyme Regis,	
E.C. Thurs **3,464**	10 A2
Lyon's Gate	11 C1
Lytchett Matravers **2,182**	12 B2
Lytchett Minster	
(with Upton **6,475**)	12 B2
Maiden Newton **785**	11 C2
Mannington	13 C1

Place		Grid Ref
Manston **184**		8 B2
Mapperton **30**		10 B2
Mappowder **195**		11 D1
Margaret Marsh **45**		8 B2
Marnhull **1,844**		8 B2
Marshwood **301**		10 A2
Martinstown		11 C2
Melbury Abbas **265**		*
Melbury Bubb **66**		11 C1
Melbury Osmond **189**		11 C1
Melbury Sampford **43**		11 C1
Melcombe Bingham		12 A1
Melcombe Horsey **153**		*
Melcombe Regis		
(with Weymouth **44,818**)		11 C3
Melplash		10 B2
Middlemarsh		11 C1
Milborne St Andrew **928**		12 A2
Milton Abbas **433**		12 A2
Milton on Stour		8 B1
Minterne Magna **196**		11 C1
Monkton Up Wimborne		9 D2
Moor Crichel **181**		12 B1
Moordown		13 C2
Morcombelake		10 B2
Morden **334**		12 B2
Moreton **285**		12 A3
Mosterton **363**		10 B1
Motcombe **860**		8 B1
Mudeford		13 D2
Netherbury **992**		10 B2
Nether Cerne **13**		11 C2
Nether Compton **336**		8 A2
Nettlecombe		10 B2
Newtown		13 C2
Norden		12 B3
North Poorton **26**		10 B2
North Wootton **44**		8 A2
Oborne **121**		8 A2
Okeford Fitzpaine **634**		8 B2
Orchard (E. & W.) **191**		8 B2
Osmington **429**		11 D3
Osmington Mills		11 D3
Over Compton **152**		*
Owermoigne **1,169**		12 A3
Pamphill **647**		*
Parkstone		13 C2
Parley Cross		13 C2
Pentridge **193**		9 D2
Piddlehinton **437**		11 D2
Piddletrenthide **610**		11 D2
Pilsdon **39**		10 B2
Pimperne **3,232**		9 C2
Plush		11 D1
Poole, E.C. Wed **119,316**		12 B2
Portesham **451**		11 C3
Portland **12,405**		10 A3
Powerstock **402**		10 B2
Poxwell **54**		12 A3
Poyntington **140**		8 A2
Preston		11 D3
Puddletown **946**		11 D2
Pulham **176**		*
Puncknowle **369**		11 C3
Purse Caundle **110**		8 A2
Rampisham **140**		11 C1
Ridge		12 B3
Rodden		11 C3
Ryall		10 B2
Ryme Intrinseca **156**		11 C1

Place		Grid Ref
St Ives (with		
St Leonard's **6,344**)		13 C1
St Leonard's (with		
St Ives **6,344**)		13 C1
Salwayash		10 B2
Sandbanks		13 C3
Sandford Orcas **183**		8 A2
Seaborough **70**		10 B1
Shaftesbury, E.C. Wed **4,951**		8 B1
Shapwick **182**		12 B1
Sherborne, E.C. Wed **7,614**		8 A2
Shillingstone **762**		8 B2
Shipton Gorge **316**		10 B2
Silton **140**		*
Sixpenny Handley **816**		9 C2
Slepe		12 B2
Southbourne		13 C2
South Perrott **220**		10 B1
Southwell		10 A3
Spetisbury **537**		12 B1
Stalbridge **2,336**		8 B2
Stalbridge Weston		8 A2
Stanbridge		12 B1
Stanton St Gabriel **101**		*
Stapehill		13 C2
Steeple **119**		12 B3
Stinsford **295**		11 D2
Stoborough		12 B3
Stoborough Green		12 B3
Stockwood **31**		*
Stoke Abbott **214**		10 B1
Stokeford		12 A3
Stoke Wake **63**		*
Stourpaine **603**		*
Stour Provost **508**		8 B2
Stour Row		8 B2
Stourton Caundle **346**		8 A2
Stratton **297**		11 C2
Stubhampton		9 C2
Studland **559**		13 C3
Sturminster Common		8 B2
Sturminster		
Marshall **1,145**		12 B2
Sturminster Newton **2,284**		8 B2
Sutton Waldron **170**		9 C2
Swanage,		
E.C. Thurs **8,822**		13 C3
Swyre **96**		10 B3
Sydling St Nicholas **322**		11 C2
Symondsbury **1,074**		10 B2
Tadden		12 B1
Tarrant Crawford **30**		12 B1
Tarrant Gunville **229**		9 C2
Tarrant Hinton **170**		9 C2
Tarrant Keyneston **309**		12 B1
Tarrant Launceston **427**		9 C2
Tarrant Monkton **1,686**		12 B1
Tarrant Rawston **55**		12 B1
Tarrant Rushton **106**		12 B1
Three Legged Cross		13 C1
Thorncombe		
(Beaminster **(599)**		10 A1
Thorncombe (Blandford F.)		12 A1
Thornford **635**		8 A2
Tincleton **109**		12 A2
Todber **127**		8 B2
Toller Fratrum **12**		11 C2
Toller Porcorum **218**		11 C2
Tolpuddle **280**		12 A2
Trent **299**		8 A2
Trickett's Cross		13 C2
Turners Puddle **41**		12 A2
Turnworth **48**		12 A1

Place		Grid Ref
Tyneham		12 B3
Up Cerne **7**		11 C1
Up Sydling		11 C1
Upton (with		
Lytchett Minster **6,475**)		12 B2
Upwey		11 C3
Verwood, E.C. Thurs **6,147**		9 D2
Walditch		10 B2
Wareham, E.C. Wed **4,596**		12 B3
Wareham St Martin **3,370**		*
Warmwell **153**		12 A3
Watercombe **312**		*
Waterloo		13 C2
West Bay		10 B2
West Bexington		10 B2
Westbourne		13 C2
West Chelborough **28**		10 B1
West Compton **18**		11 C2
West Holme		12 B3
West Knighton **376**		11 D3
West Lulworth **910**		12 A3
West Milton		10 B2
West Moors,		
E.C. Wed **6,617**		13 C1
Weston		10 A3
West Parley,		
E.C. Wed **3,611**		13 C2
West Stafford **258**		11 D2
West Stour **133**		8 B1
Weymouth, E.C. Wed and		
Melcombe Regis **44,818**		11 D3
Whatcombe		12 A2
Whitcombe **26**		*
Whitechurch		
Canonicorum **613**		10 A2
White Lackington		11 D2
Wick		13 C2
Wimborne Minster,		
E.C. Wed **5,554**		12 B2
Wimborne St Giles **366**		9 D2
Winfrith Newburgh **602**		12 A3
Winterborne Carne **54**		*
Winterborne Clenston **68**		12 A1
Winterborne Herrington **27**		11 D3
Winterborne Houghton **176**		12 A2
Winterborne Kingston **491**		12 A2
Winterborne Monkton **64**		11 C3
Winterborne St Martin **592**		*
Winterborne Stickland **559**		12 A1
Winterborne		
Whitechurch **559**		12 A2
Winterborne Zelston **122**		12 B2
Winterbourne Abbas **163**		11 C2
Winterbourne		
Steepleton **235**		11 C2
Winton		13 C2
Witchampton **398**		12 B1
Woodlands **463**		13 C1
Woodsford **292**		12 A2
Woodyates		9 D2
Wool, E.C. Thurs **5,219**		12 A3
Woolland **77**		12 A1
Wootton Fitzpaine **331**		10 A2
Worth Matravers **525**		12 B3
Wraxall **40**		*
Wyke		8 B1
Wyke Regis		10 A3
Wynford Eagle **53**		11 C2
Yetminster **898**		8 A2

Population figures are based upon the 1981 census and relate to the local authority area or parish, as constituted at that date. Places with no population figure form part of a larger local authority area or parish. Population figures in bold type.

E.C. Early Closing   *Parish not shown on maps pages 8-13 due to limitation of scale.

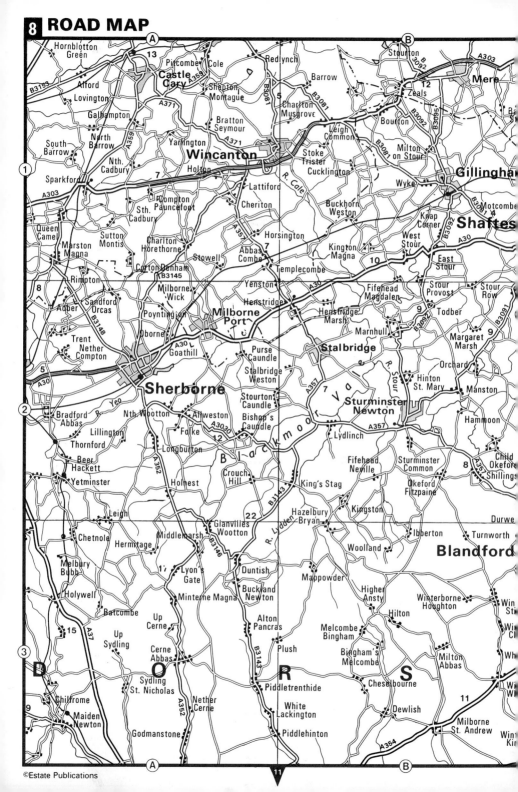

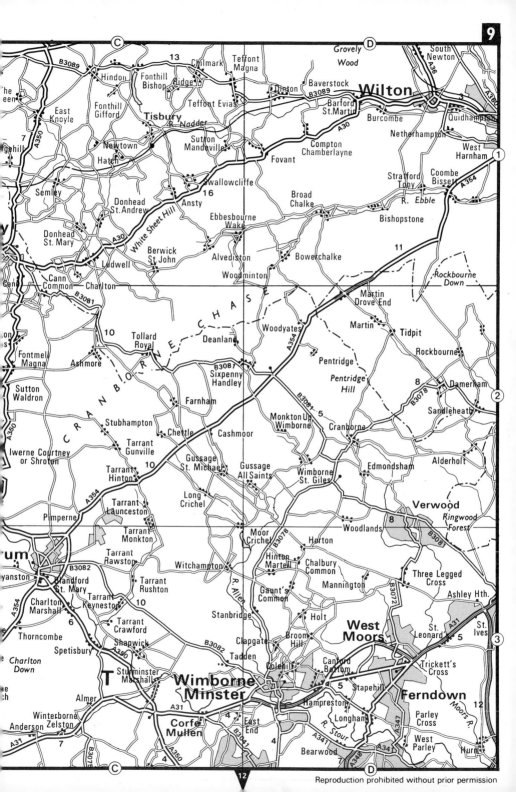

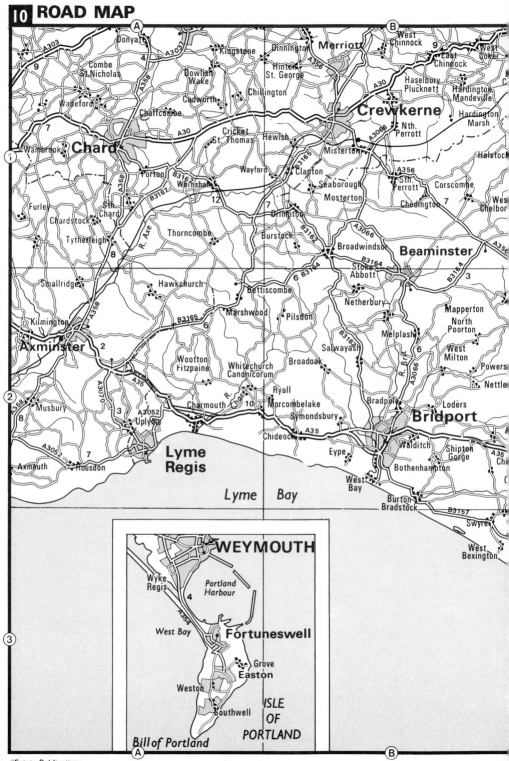

©Estate Publications

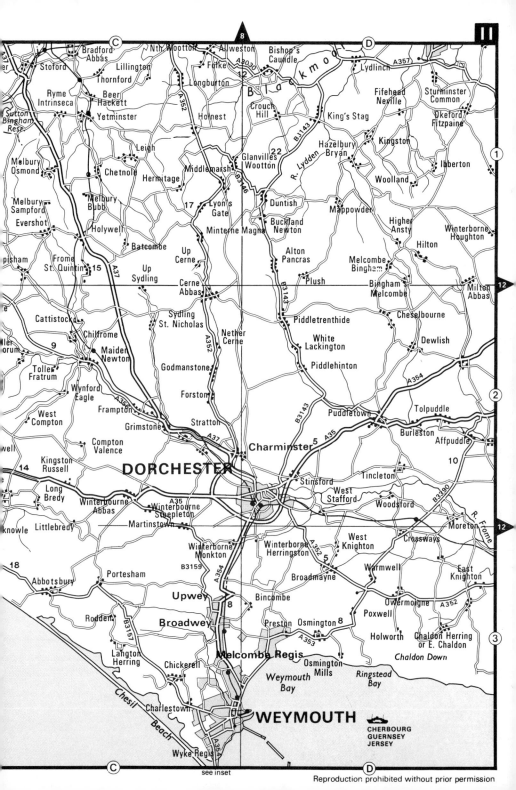

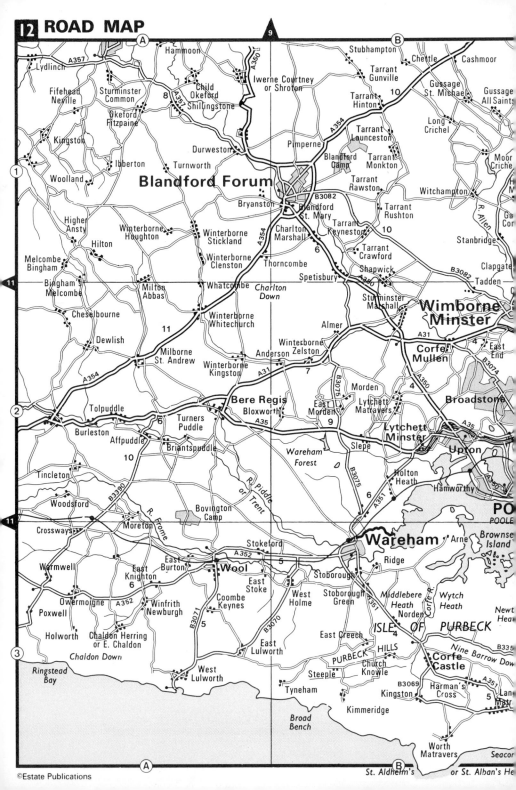

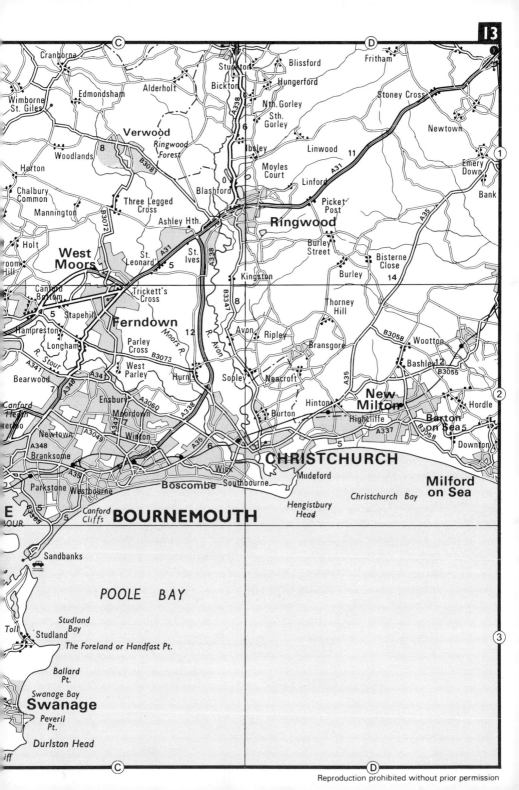

Ⓒ Ⓓ

Cranborne
Blissford
Fritham

Wimborne
St. Giles
Edmondsham
Alderholt
Stukeley
Bickton
Hungerford
Stoney Cross
① ①

Verwood
Nth. Gorley
Sth. Gorley
Newtown

Woodlands
Ringwood
Forest
8
Horton
Ibsley
Linwood
11
Emery
Down

Chalbury
Common
Mannington
Three Legged
Cross
Ashley Hth.
Blashford
Moyles
Court
Linford
Picket
Post
Bank

Holt
Ringwood
Burley
Street
Bisterne
Close

West
Moors
St.
Leonard
St.
Ives
Kingston
Burley
14

Canford
Bottom
Trickett's
Cross
Ferndown
Thorney
Hill
Wootton

Stapehill
Avon
Ripley
Bashley
12

Hampreston
Longham
Parley
Cross
West
Parley
Hurn
Sopley
Bransgore
New
Milton
Hordle

Bearwood
Ensbury
Moordown
Hinton
Highcliffe
Barton
on Sea
Downton

Canford
Heath
Newtown
Winton
Burton
CHRISTCHURCH

Branksome
Wick
Mudeford
Milford
on Sea

Parkstone
Westbourne
Boscombe
Southbourne
Christchurch Bay

Canford
Cliffs
BOURNEMOUTH
Hengistbury
Head

Sandbanks

POOLE BAY

Studland
Bay
Toll
Studland
The Foreland or Handfast Pt.
③

Ballard
Pt.
Swanage Bay
Swanage
Peveril
Pt.

Durlston Head

Ⓒ Ⓓ

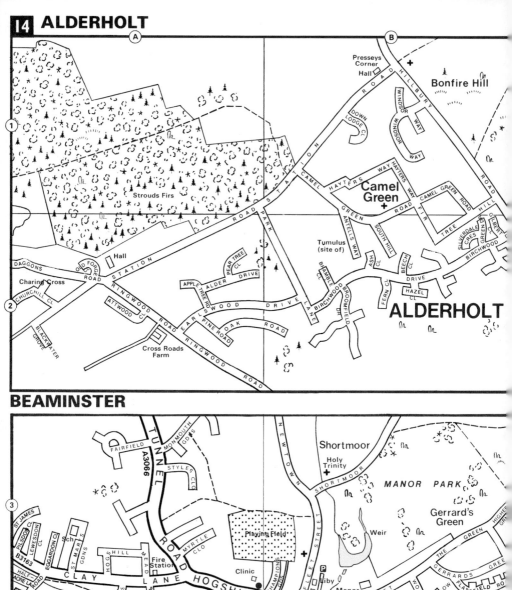

BEAMINSTER

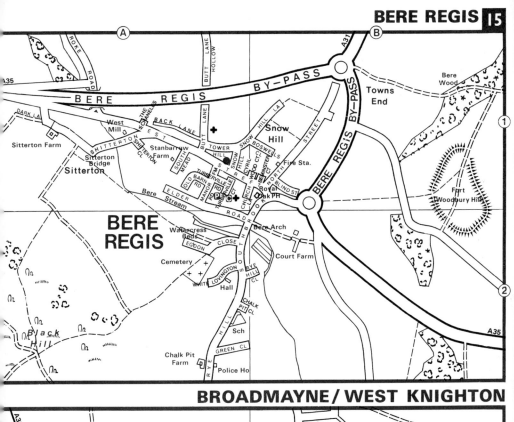

BROADMAYNE / WEST KNIGHTON

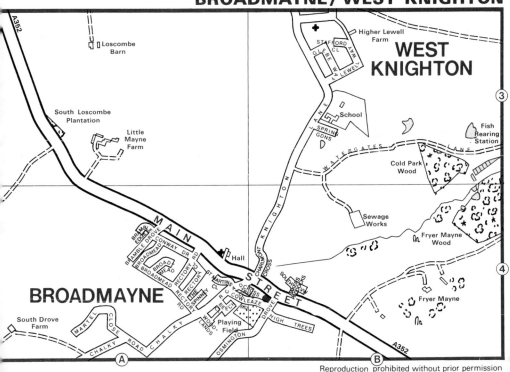

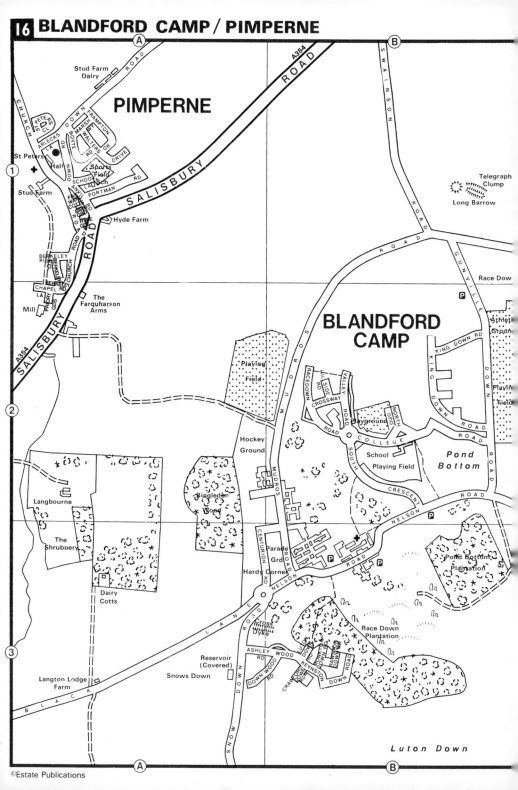

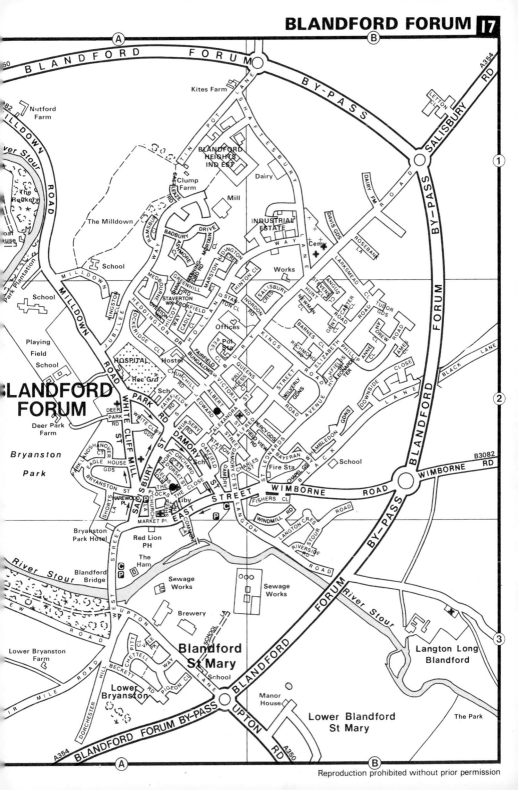

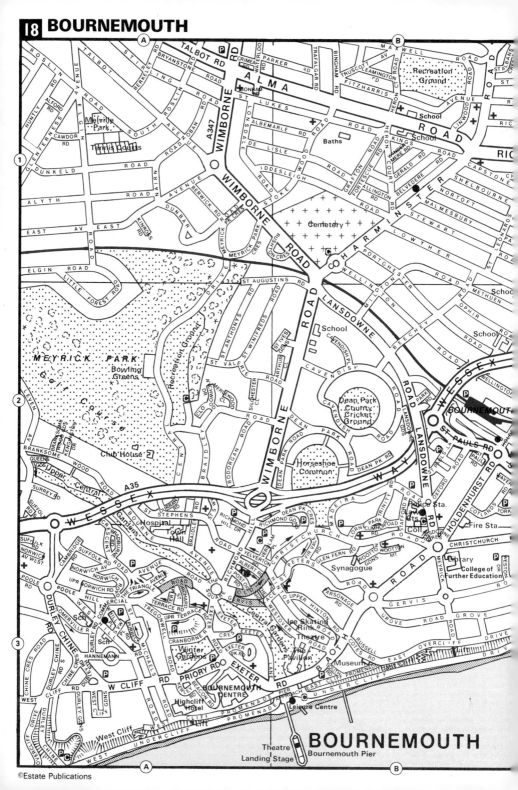

18 BOURNEMOUTH

BOURNEMOUTH

©Estate Publications

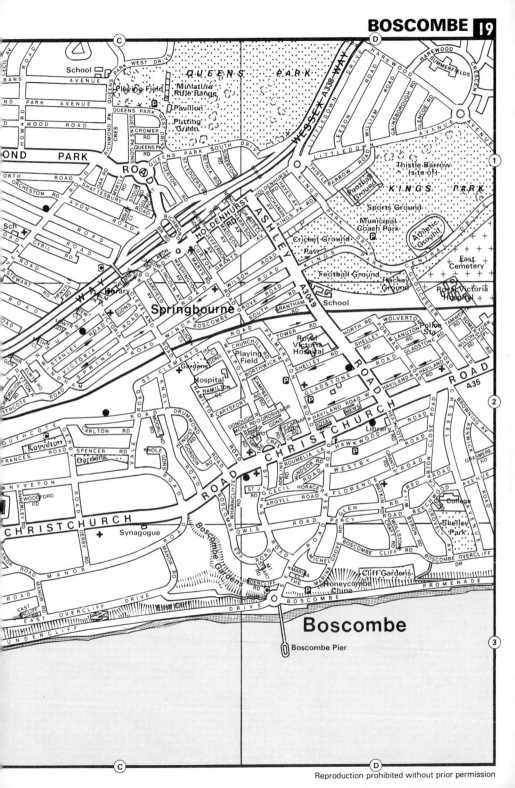

Boscombe

Boscombe Pier

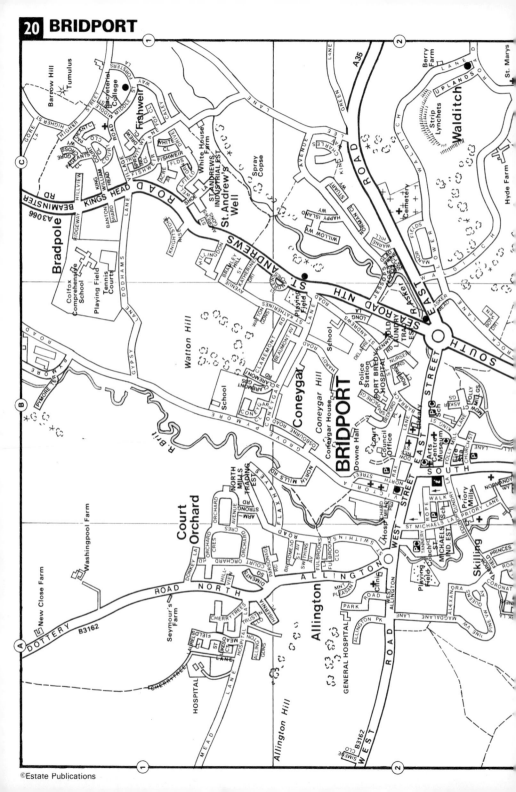

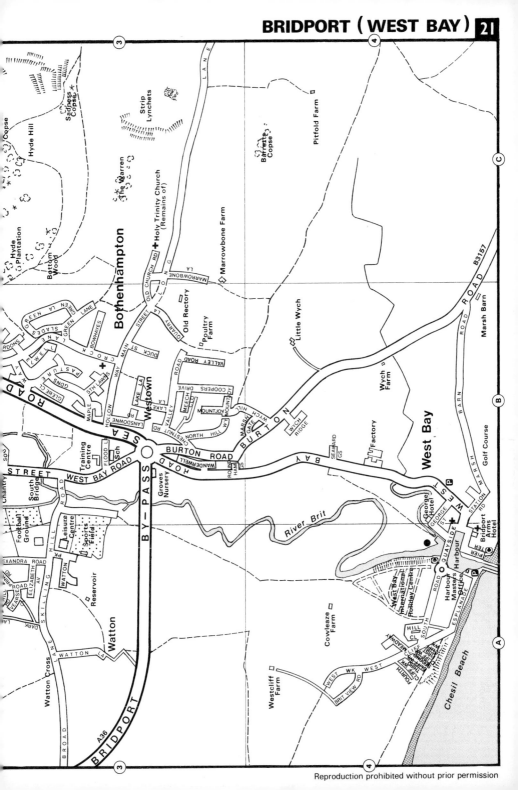

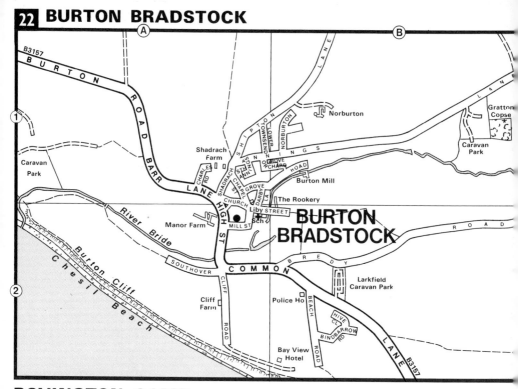

BURTON BRADSTOCK

B3157

BURTON ROAD BARR LANE

Caravan Park

Caravan Park

Gratton Copse

Caravan Park

Norburton

Shadrach Farm

Burton Mill

The Rookery

Manor Farm

BURTON BRADSTOCK

River Bride

Burton Cliff

Chesil Beach

SOUTHOVER

COMMON

Cliff Farm

Police Ho

Larkfield Caravan Park

Bay View Hotel

B3157

BOVINGTON CAMP

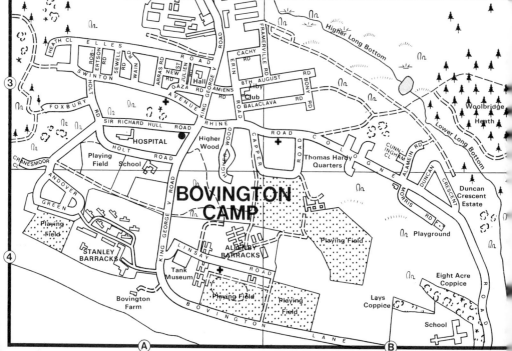

Higher Long Bottom

Lower Long Bottom

Woolbridge Heath

HOSPITAL

Higher Wood

Thomas Hardy Quarters

Duncan Crescent Estate

Playing Field

School

BOVINGTON CAMP

Playground

Playing Field

STANLEY BARRACKS

ALDENEY BARRACKS

Tank Museum

Playing Field

Playing Field

Eight Acre Coppice

Lays Coppice

School

Bovington Farm

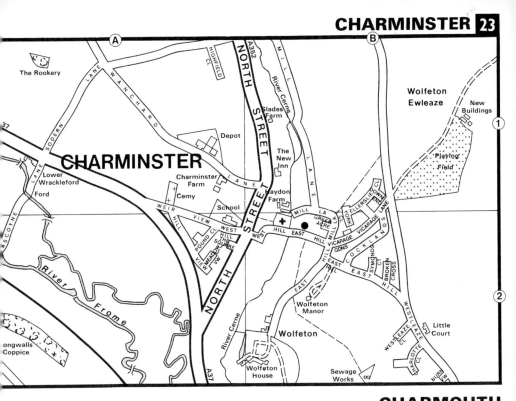

CHARMINSTER

The Rookery

Wolfeton Ewleaze

New Buildings

Slades Farm

Depot

The New Inn

Playlog Field

Lower Wrackleford

Ford

Charminster Farm

Cemy

School

Jaydon Farm

Green Acre

Ellerslie

York

Vicarage

Vicarage Lane

Downe

Cockland

Symonds

Broken Cross

Little Court

Hill Square

Hill Meadow

Pound Cl

West View

Weir

West View

Hill East

Vicarage Gdns

East Hill

East

Westleaze Cl

Westleaze

Charlotte Cl

Bush

River Frome

Longwalls Coppice

River Cerne

Wolfeton Manor

Wolfeton

Wolfeton House

Sewage Works

CHARMOUTH

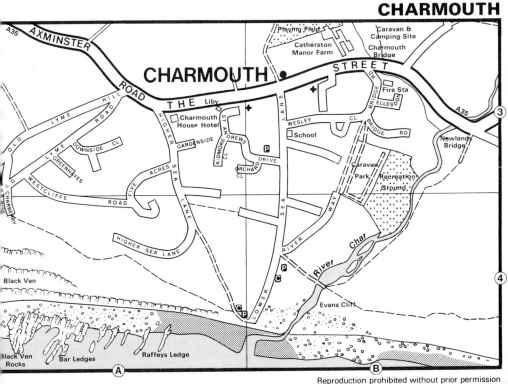

Playing Field

Catherston Manor Farm

Caravan & Camping Site

Charmouth Bridge

CHARMOUTH

Liby

Charmouth House Hotel

Fire Sta

Elleso

Wesley

School

Bridge Rd

Newlands Bridge

Axminster Road

Lyme Hill Road

Old Lyme Road

Downside Cl

Greenhayes

Westcliffe Road

Gardenside

St Andrews

Kidmore Cl

Orchard Cl

Drive

Five Acres

Higher Sea Lane

The Street

Bridge Rd

Caravan Park

Recreation Ground

River Char

Lower Sea Lane

River Way

Black Ven

Black Ven Rocks

Bar Ledges

Raffeys Ledge

Evans Cliff

Charberry

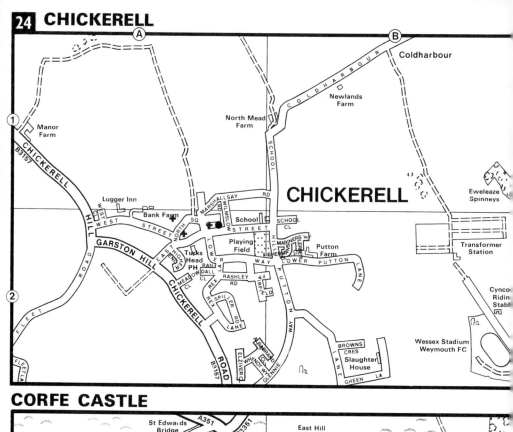

CHICKERELL

Coldharbour

Newlands Farm

North Mead Farm

Eweleaze Spinneys

Manor Farm

B3157

CHICKERELL HILL

Lugger Inn

Bank Farm

WEST STREET

School

SCHOOL CL

Transformer Station

GARSTON HILL

Tucks Head PH

Playing Field

MARINERS

FISHERMANS

Putton Farm

LOWER PUTTON LANE

Cynco Ridin Stabl

CHICKERELL ROAD B3157

RASHLEY RD

SPILLER RD LANE

PUTTON WAY

BROWNS CRES

Slaughter House

GREEN LA

Wessex Stadium Weymouth FC

FLEET

CORFE CASTLE

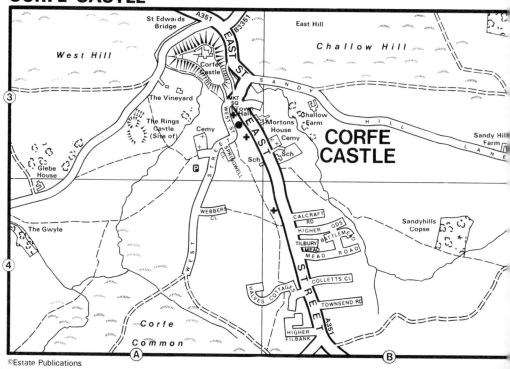

St Edwards Bridge

A351

B3351

EAST ST

East Hill

Challow Hill

West Hill

Corfe Castle

SANDY

The Vineyard

MKT SQ

Town Hall

Challow Farm

HILL

Sandy Hill Farm

The Rings Castle (Site of)

Cemy

WEST ST

Mortons House

Cemy

CORFE CASTLE

SANDY HILL LANE

Glebe House

P

Sch

Sch

SPRINGWELL

The Gwyle

WEBBERS CL

CALCRAFT RD

HIGHER TILBURY MEAD

BATTLEMEAD

GDS

Sandyhills Copse

WEST STREET

MEAD ROAD

HALVES COTTAGES

COLLETTS CL

STREET

A351

TOWNSEND RD

Corfe Common

HIGHER FILBANK

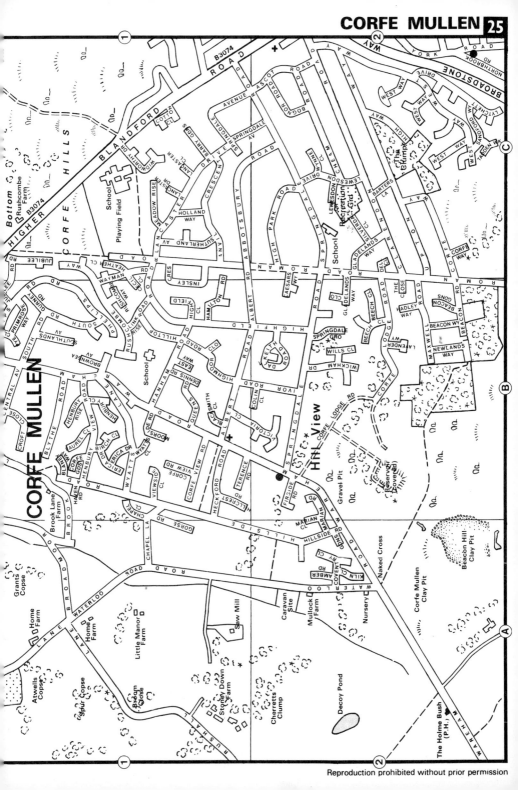

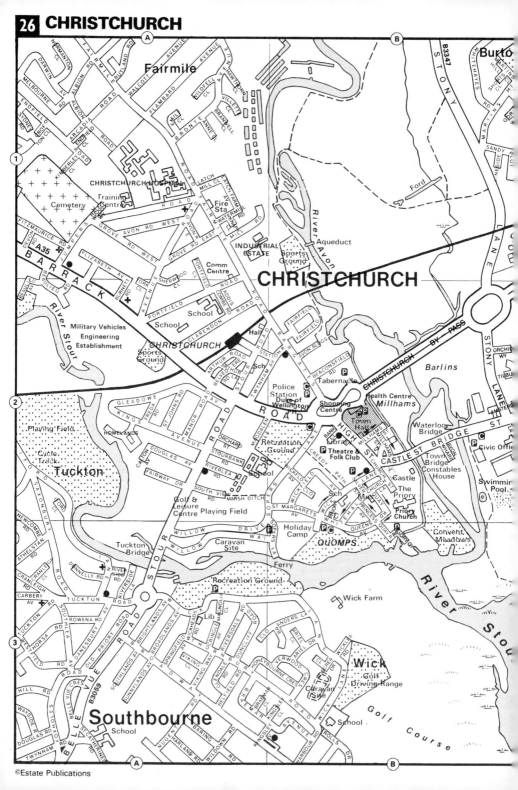

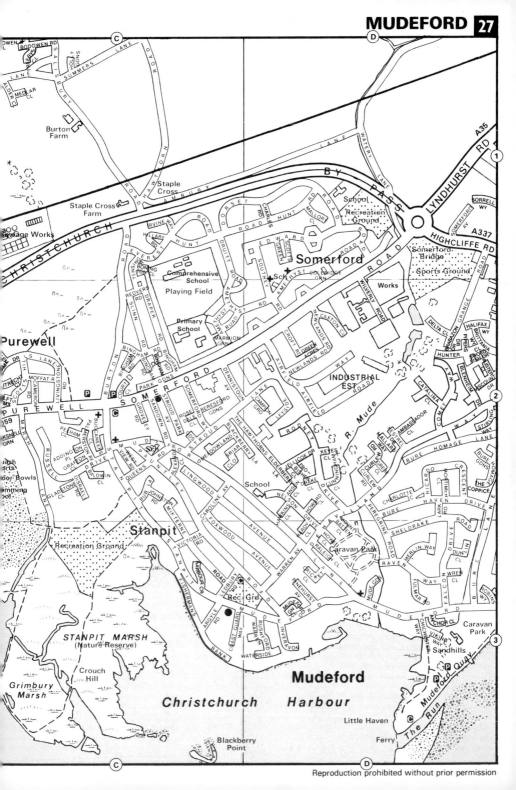

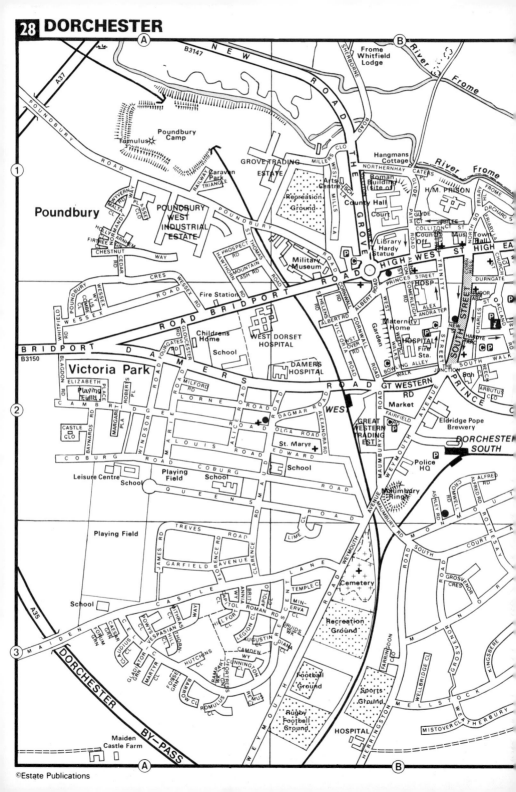

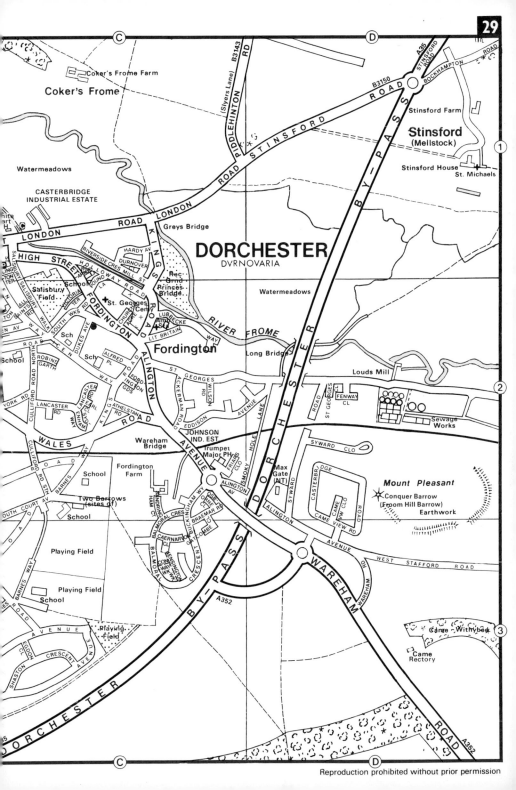

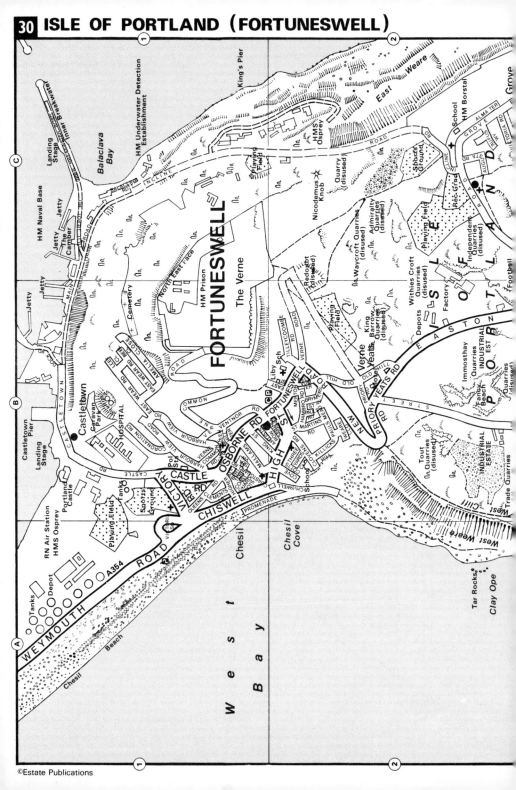

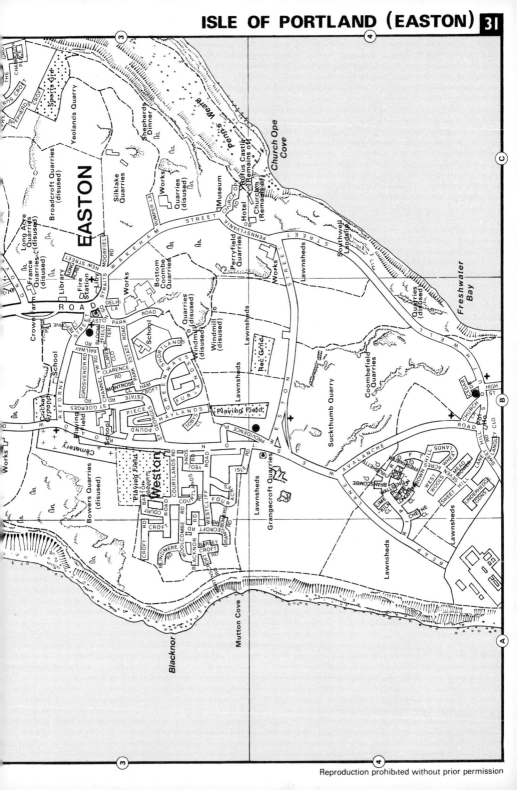

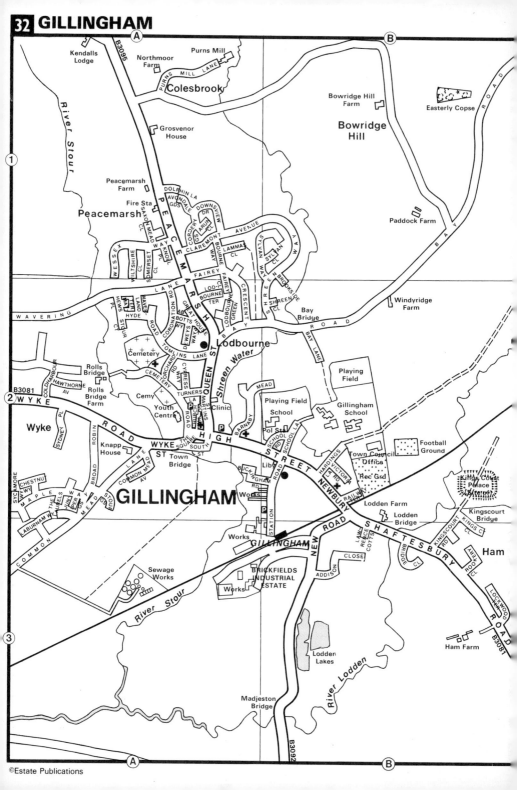

Kendalls Lodge

Northmoor Farm

Purns Mill

PURNS MILL LANE

Colesbrook

B3095

Grosvenor House

Bowridge Hill Farm

Easterly Copse

Bowridge Hill

ROAD

Peacemarsh Farm

Fire Sta

DOLPHIN LA

AVONDALE GDS

DOWNSVIEW

Peacemarsh

SAXON MEAD CL

WESSEX CL

WILTSHIRE CL

SOMERSET CL

KNOLL

WAY

LANE

CORSLEY DR

LARUN

CLAREMONT

LAMMAS CL

FAIREY WAY

BOURNE WAY

FAIREY

CRESCENT

SYLVAN

NYATS

BROOKSIDE

SHREEN

CLAREMONT

AVENUE

Paddock Farm

BAY

Windyridge Farm

WAVERING

HEWS CT

STOUR CL

LANE

MAYBE

HYDE

CORONATION RD

GREAT HOUSE

ABBOTS

TOMLINS LANE

CYPRESS RD

ORCHARD WAY

DEWEYS WAY

LOD TER

BOURNE

LODBOURNE GREEN

QUEEN ST

SHREEN CL

SHREENDE

Bay Bridge

ROAD

BAY LANE

Lodbourne

Shreen Water

Cemetery

Rolls Bridge

HAWTHORNE AV

Rolls Bridge Farm

COLDHARBOUR

Cemy

CEMETERY

TURNERS CL

Youth Centre

LA

Clinic

BARNABY

Playing Field School

MEAD

Playing Field

Gillingham School

Playing Field

B3081

WYKE

ROAD

Wyke

SYDNEY PL

ROBIN

Knapp House

BROAD

STOUR MEAD

COMMON MEAD

LANE

WYKE ST

THE SQUARE

SOUTH ST

Town Bridge

HIGH

STREET

SCHOOL RD

SCHOOL LA

HARDINGS

Pol Stn

VICTORY RD

Town Council Office

Rec Grd

Football Ground

Kings Court Peace Memorial

SYCAMORE

WAY

CHESTNUT WAY

MAPLE

LAURELS

THE

JUNIPER WAY

LABURNAM WAY

COMMON

GILLINGHAM

BUCKINGHAM RD

STATION RD

Libv

P

Works

P

NEWBURY

RAILWAY

Lodden Farm

Lodden Bridge

KINGSCOURT RD

KINGS CL

Kingscourt Bridge

KINGS CL

OAKEN

Ham

Works

GILLINGHAM

NEW ROAD

SHAFTESBURY

LANE

REECE

COTTS

BRIDGE CL

ADDISON

CLOSE

Sewage Works

BRICKFIELDS INDUSTRIAL ESTATE

Works

River Stour

Lodden Lakes

River Lodden

Madjeston Bridge

Ham Farm

LOCKWOOD

ROAD

B3081

B3092

River Stour

©Estate Publications

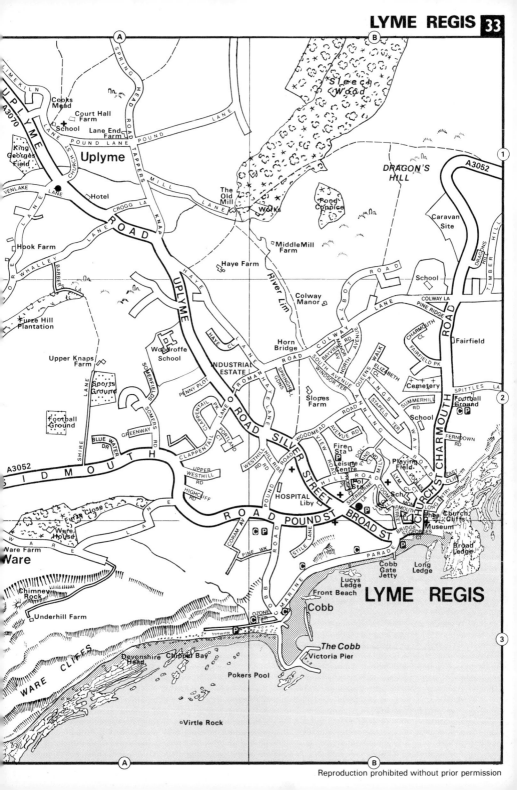

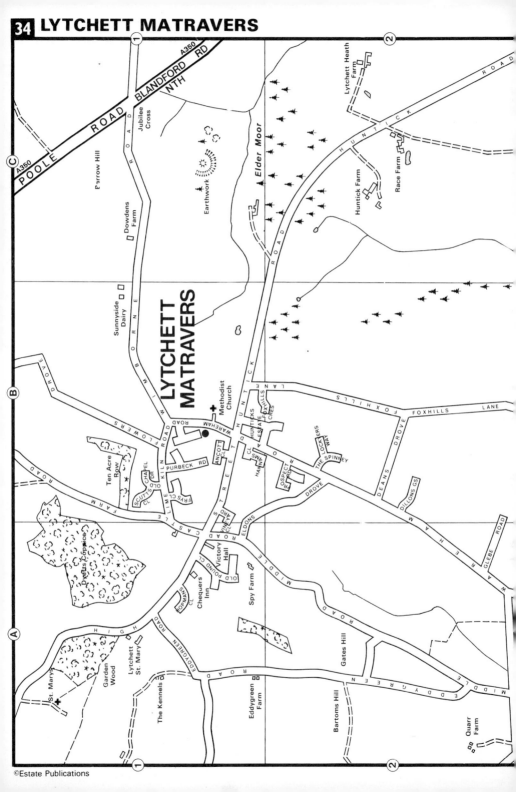

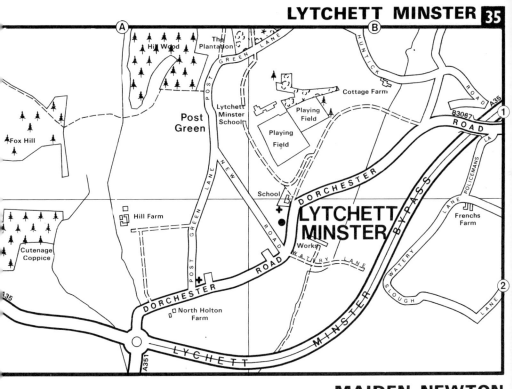

MAIDEN NEWTON

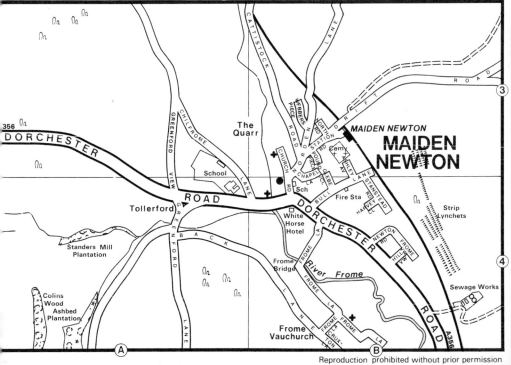

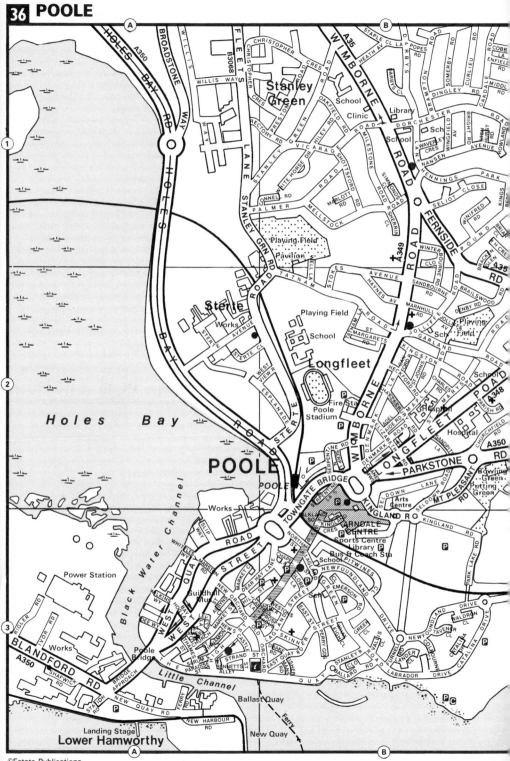

PUDDLETOWN

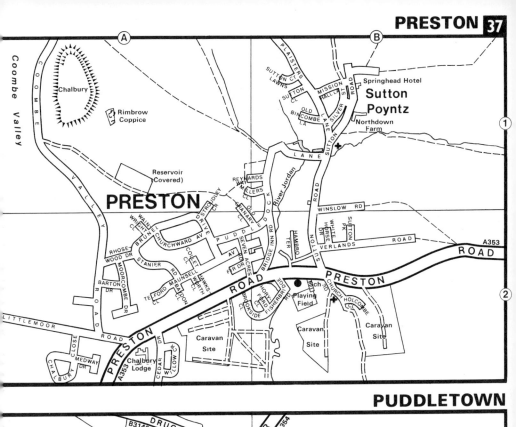

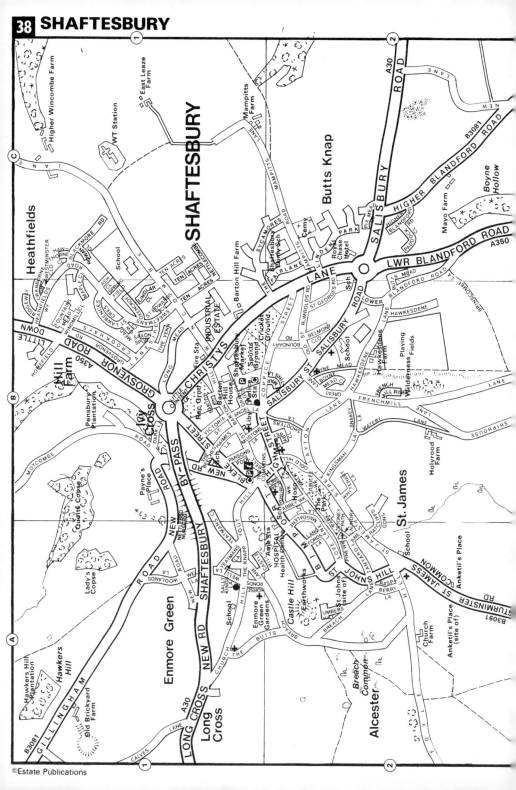

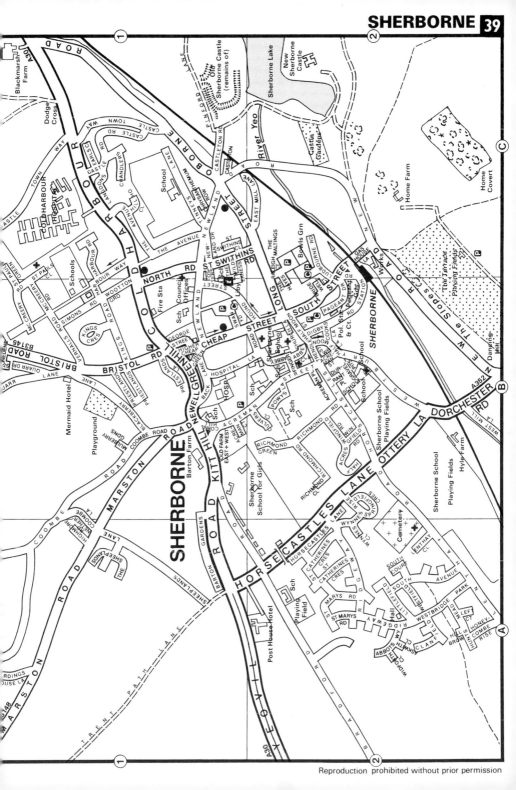

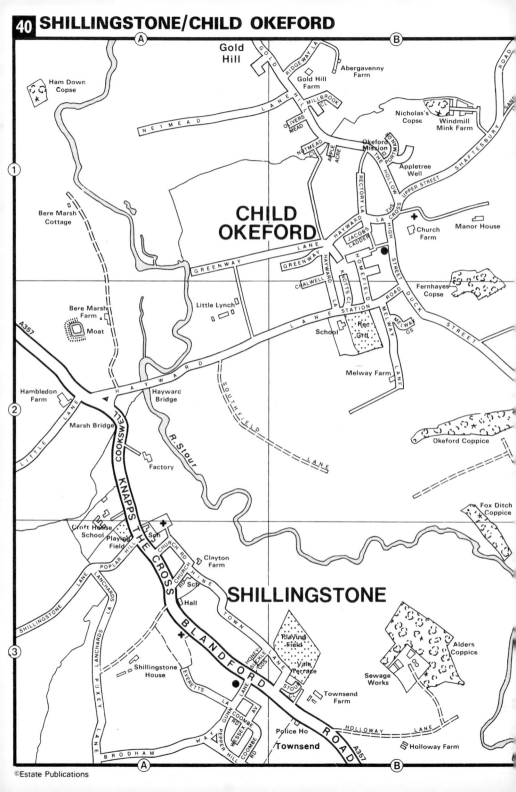

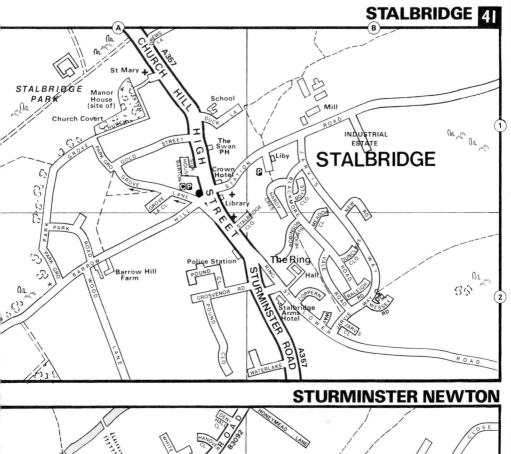

STALBRIDGE

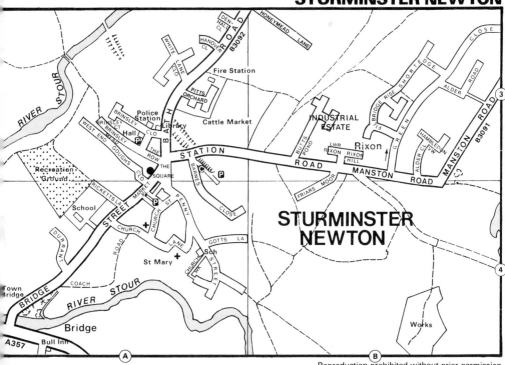

STURMINSTER NEWTON

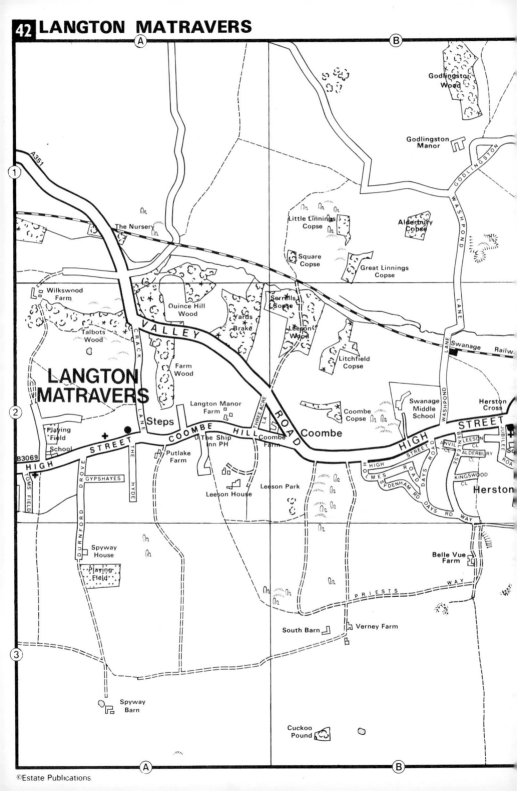

42 LANGTON MATRAVERS

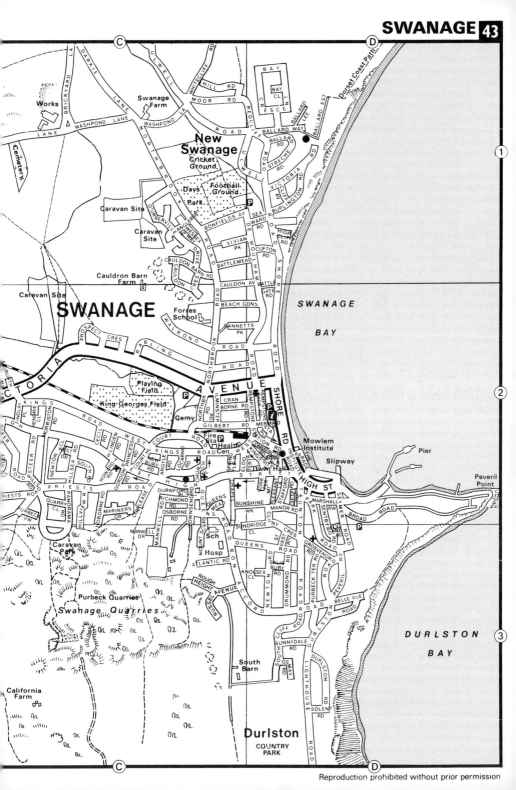

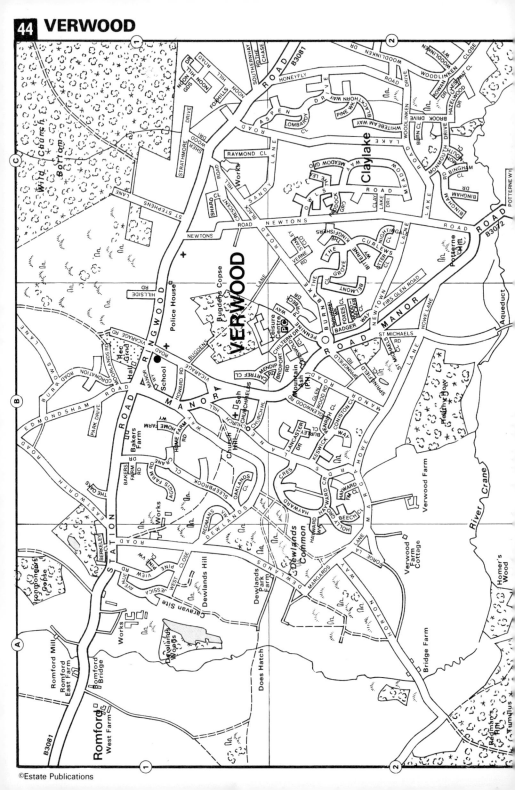

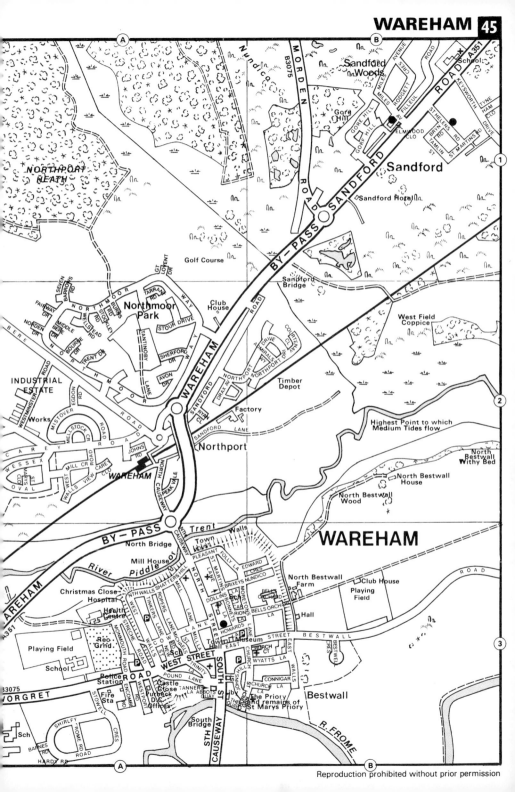

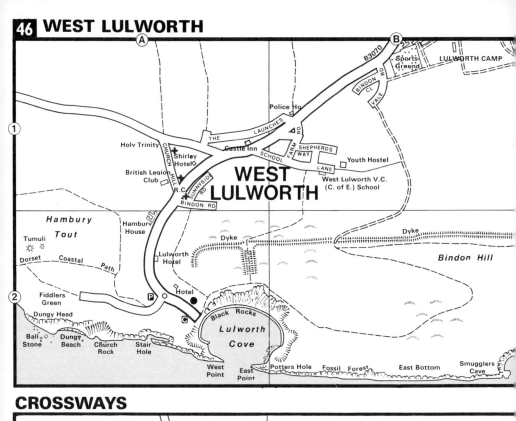

WEST LULWORTH

Holy Trinity
Shirley Hotel
British Legion Club
Hambury House
Hambury Tout
Tumuli
Dorset Coastal Path
Fiddlers Green
Dungy Head
Ball Stone
Dungy Beach
Church Rock
Stair Hole
West Point
East Point
Lulworth Hotel
Hotel
Black Rocks
Lulworth Cove
Potters Hole
Fossil Forest
East Bottom
Smugglers Cave
Bindon Hill
Dyke
Castle Inn
Police Hq
Sports Ground
LULWORTH CAMP
B3070
Bindon Cl
Vale Rd
Shepherds Way
Lane
School
Farm Rd
The Launches
Church Hill
Sunnyside Rd
Bindon Rd
Youth Hostel
West Lulworth V.C. (C. of E.) School
R.C.

CROSSWAYS

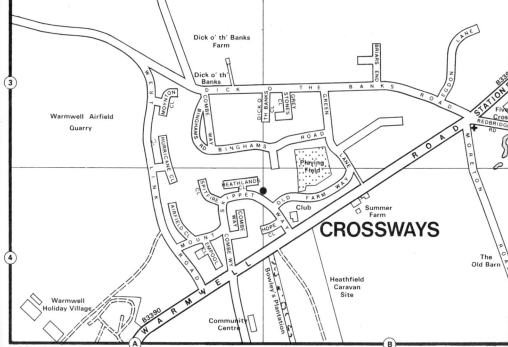

CROSSWAYS

Dick o' th' Banks Farm
Dick o' th' Banks
Warmwell Airfield Quarry
Briars End
Egdon Lane
B3390
STATION
Five Cross
Redbridge Rd
West Link
Avon Cl
Hurricane Cl
Binghams Rd
Combe Way
Dick O Th Banks Cl
Grey Stones Cl
The Green
Banks Road
Binghams Road
Moreton Road
Playing Field
Spitfire Cl
Tippet Cl
Heathlands Cl
Old Farm Way
Green Lane
Airfield Court
Combe Way
Empool Cl
Combe Way
Hope Cl
Way
Club
Summer Farm
The Old Barn
Warmwell Holiday Village
B3390
Community Centre
Bowley's Plantation
Heathfield Caravan Site
Warmwell

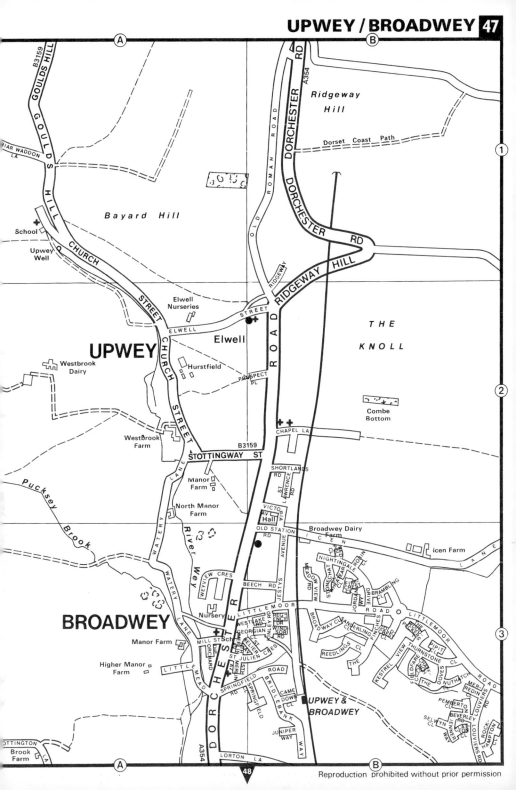

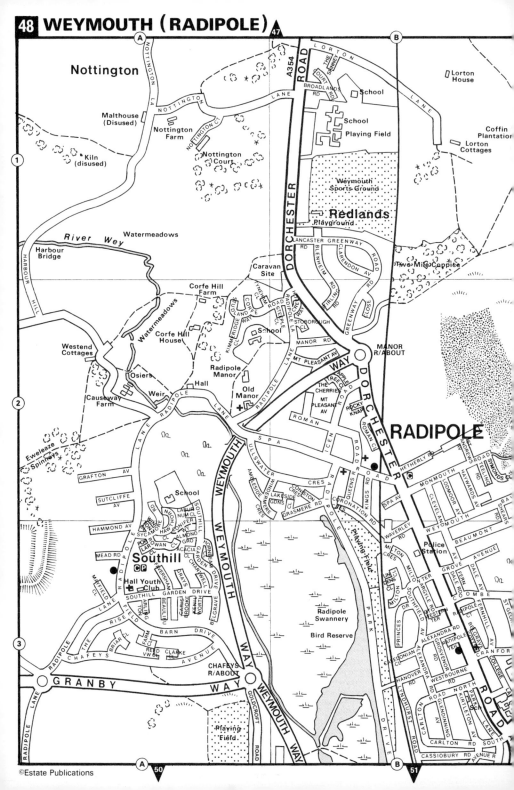

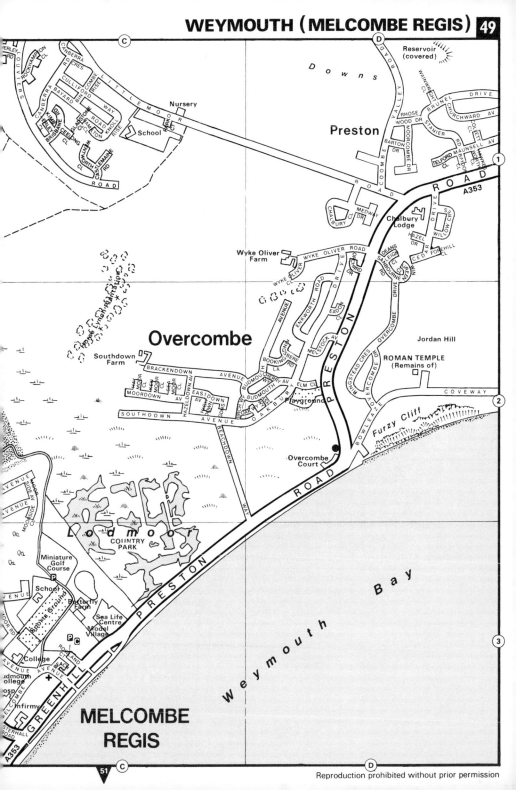

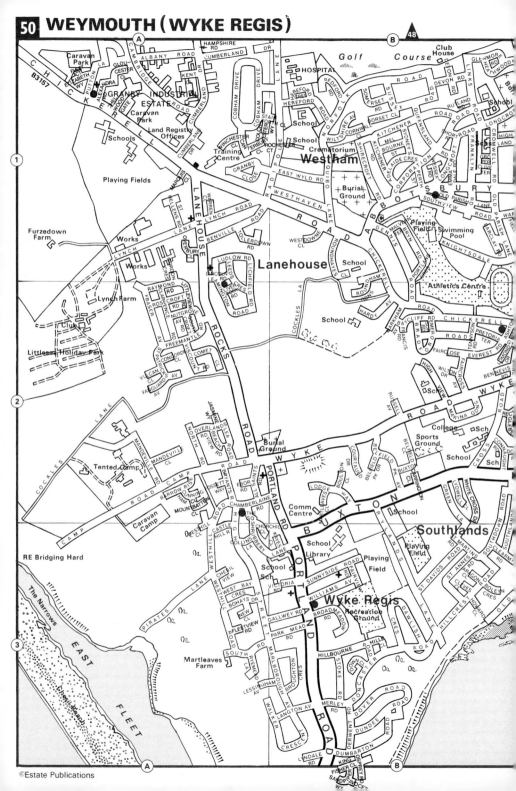

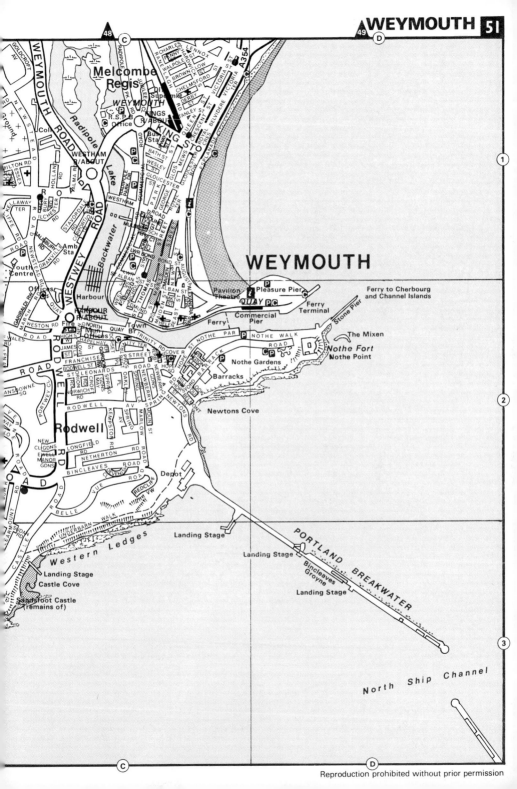

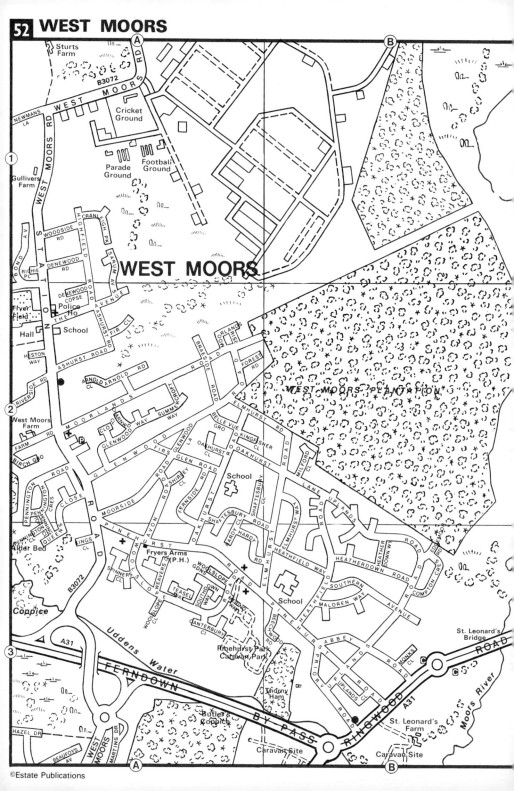

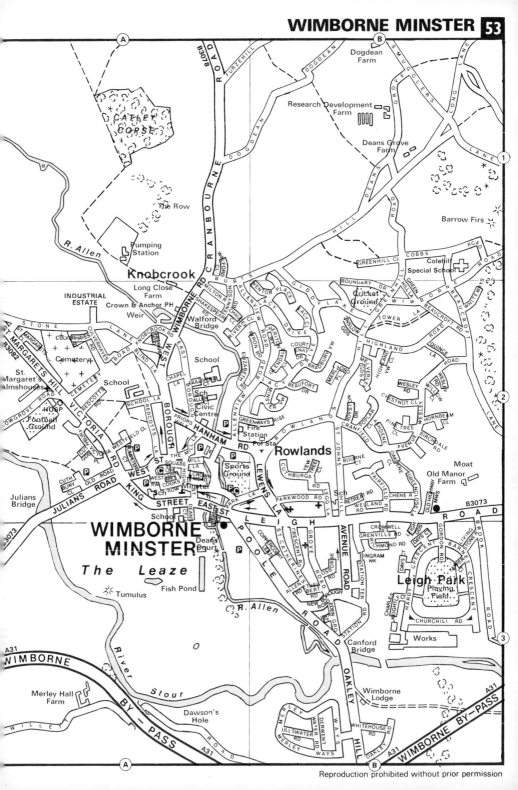

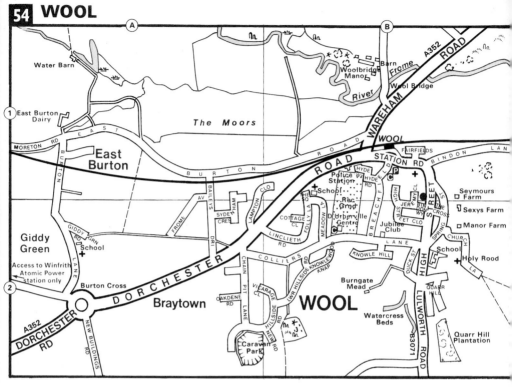

INDEX TO STREETS

Road marked * do not
appear on the map, due to
lack of space.
Their location will be found
in the vicinity of the name
following them in the index.

ALDERHOLT

Alder Dri	14 A2
Antells Way	14 B2
Apple Tree Rd	14 A2
Ash Clo	14 B2
Attwood Clo	14 A2
Beech Clo	14 B2
Birchwood Dri	14 B2
Blackwater Gro	14 A2
Bramble Clo	14 B2
Broomfield Dri	14 B2
Camel Green Rd	14 B1
Churchill Clo	14 A2
Daggons Rd	14 A2
Down Lodge Clo	14 B1
Earlswood Dri	14 B1
Fern Clo	14 B2
Fir Tree Hill	14 B1
Gilbert Clo	14 B2
Green Dri	14 B2
Hayters Way	14 B1
Hazel Clo	14 B2
Hillbury Rd	14 B1
Oak Rd	14 A2
Old Forge Clo	14 A2
Park La	14 B2
Pear Tree Clo	14 A2
Pine Rd	14 A2
Ringwood Rd	14 A2
Silverdale Cres	14 B2
South Hill	14 B2
Station Rd	14 A2
Windsor Way	14 B1

BEAMINSTER

Barnes La	14 A4
Bridport Rd	14 B4
Champions	14 B3

Champions Gdns	14 B3
Church St	14 A4
Clay La	14 A3
Culverhayes	14 A4
East St	14 B4
Eggardon Clo	14 A3
Fairfield	14 A3
Flatsfield Rd	14 B3
Fleet St	14 B3
Gerrards Grn	14 B3
Glebe Ct	14 A4
Greens Cross Dri	14 A4
Half-Acre La	14 A3
Higher Grn	14 B3
Hogshill Mead	14 A3
Hogshill St	14 A3
Hollymoor Clo	14 B4
Hollymoor Common	14 B4
Hollymoor Gdns	14 B4
Lewesden Clo	14 A3
Manor Gdns	14 B4
Monmouth Gdns	14 A3
Myrtle Clo	14 A3
Newetown	14 B3
North St	14 B4
Pilsdon Clo	14 A3
Prout Hill	14 B4
Riverside	14 B4
St James	14 A3
St Mary Well St	14 A4
St Marys Gdns	14 A3
Shadrack St	14 A4
Shortmoor	14 B3
Shorts La	14 A4
Stoke Rd	14 A4
Styles Clo	14 A3
Tanyard	14 A4
The Green	14 B3
The Square	14 B4
Tunnel Rd	14 A3
Whitcombe Rd	14 B4
Willow Gro	14 B4
Woodswater La	14 B3

BERE REGIS

Back La	15 A1

Beaminster Ct	15 B1
Bere Regis By-Pass	15 A1
Blind St	15 B1
Boswell Clo	15 B1
Butt La	15 A1
Butt Lane Hollow	15 A1
Chalk Pit Clo	15 A2
Church La	15 A1
Cyril Wood Ct	15 B1
Dark La	15 A1
Egdon Clo	15 A2
Elder Rd	15 A1
Green Clo	15 A2
Manor Farm Rd	15 A1
North St	15 B1
Old Barn Rd	15 A1
Roke Rd	15 A1
Rye Hill	15 A2
Rye Hill Clo	15 A2
Shitterton	15 A1
Shitterton Clo	15 A1
Snow Hill	15 A1
Snow Hill La	15 A1
South Mead	15 A1
Southbrook	15 A2
The Chaneles	15 A1
Tower Hill	15 A1
Turberville Ct	15 A1
Turberville Rd	15 A1
West St	15 A1
White Lovington	15 A2

BLANDFORD CAMP PIMPERNE

Anvil Rd	16 A1
Arlecks La	16 A1
Ashley Wood Rd	16 A3
Barr Gro	16 A1
Berkeley Clo	16 A1
Berkeley Rise	16 A1
Berkeley Road	16 A2
Black La	16 A3
Boyte Rd	16 A1

Centurion Rd	16 A
Chapel La	16 A
Church Rd	16 A
College Rd	16 B
Crawford Down Rd	16 B
Crossway	16 B
Down Rd	16 A
Down Wood Rd	16 A
Five Way Cotts	16 A
Frampton Rd	16 A
Gunville Down Rd	16 B
Hillside Rd	16 B
Hyde Gdns	16 A
Keynston Down Rd	16 B
King Down Rd	16 B
Luton Down Rd	16 B
Marsh Way	16 A
Monkton Down Rd	16 B
Mudros Rd	16 B
Nelson Rd	16 B
North Gro	16 B
Portman Rd	16 A
Priory Gdns	16 A
Racedown Rd	16 A
Rawston Down Rd	16 A
St Peters Clo	16 A
Salisbury Rd	16 A
School La	16 A
Snow Down Rd	16 A
South Cres	16 B
Swainson Rd	16 B
Valley Rd	16 B
Walters Dri	16 A

BLANDFORD FORUM

Albert St	17 A
Alexandra St	17 A
Alfred St	17 A
Andrew Clo	17 B
Angus Clo	17 B
Anne Clo	17 B
Ashmore Clo	17 A
Badbury Dri	17 A

rnes Clo	17 B2
yfran Way	17 B2
ckett Rd	17 A3
ack La	17 B2
andford Forum	
By-Pass	17 A1
yanston St	17 A2
dley Clo	17 A2
rter Clo	17 B2
apel Gdns	17 B2
arles St	17 A2
ettell Way	17 A3
urch La	17 A2
urchill Rd	17 A2
mmon La	17 A3
iry Fm	17 B1
mory	17 A2
mory Ct St	17 A2
mory St	17 A2
vis Gdns	17 B1
er Park Rd	17 A2
rchester Hill	17 A3
rset St	17 A2
wnside Clo	17 B2
gle House Gdns	17 A2
st St	17 A2
ast Street La,	
The Close	17 A2
stleaze Rd	17 A1
ward St	17 A2
zabeth Rd	17 B2
r Mile Rd	17 A3
rfield Bungalows	17 A2
rfield Rd	17 A2
ld View Rd	17 B2
lds Oak	17 A2
hers Clo	17 B2
xfield	17 A2
nt Clo	17 B2
eenhill Rd	17 A1
mbledon Gdns	17 B2
nover Ct	17 A2
ddington Dri	17 A2
ghfields	17 B2
cot Way	17 A2
nton Clo	17 A2
lland Way	17 A2
nt Rd	17 B2
nes Clo	17 A2
bilee Way	17 A2
gs Rd	17 B2
gston Clo	17 A2
ngton Cres	17 B3
gton Rd	17 A2
ksmead Clo	17 B1
ton Clo	17 B1
ington Cres	17 A1
ckeridge Clo	17 A2
nningford Rd	17 A1
rket Pl	17 A3
rston Clo	17 A2
dbourne	17 A1
ldown	17 A1
ldown Rd	17 A1
rtain Clo	17 A1
w Rd	17 A3
wman Clo	17 B2
rdon Rd	17 B2
th Pl	17 A2
rsery Rd	17 A2
kfield St	17 A2
chard St	17 A2
k Lands	17 A2
k Rd	17 A2
el Clo	17 A2
cy Gdns	17 B2
ilip Rd	17 B2
eon Clo	17 A3
Clo	17 A3
ncess Ct	17 A2
eens Rd	17 A2
nsbury Clo	17 A1
hmond Rd	17 B2
erside Rd	17 B3
sebank La	17 B1
eonards Av	17 B2
eonards Ter	17 B2
isbury Cres	17 B2
isbury Rd	17 A2
isbury St	17 A2
ool La	17 A3
aftesbury La	17 A1
aw Clo	17 A2
eep Market Hill	17 A2
orts La	17 A2
nton Clo	17 A2
tion Ct	17 A2
verton Walk	17 A2

Stevens Clo	17 B2
Stour Rd	17 B3
The Close	17 A2
The Plocks	17 A2
*The Tabernacle,	
Sheep Market Hill	17 A2
Tin Pot La	17 A1
Tudor Gdns	17 B2
Upton La	17 A3
Upton Rd	17 A3
Vale Pk	17 A3
Victoria Rd	17 A2
*Wessex Ct, Orchard St	17 A2
West St	17 A3
White Cliff Gdns	17 A2
White Cliff Mill St	17 A2
Wilverly Gdns	17 B2
Wimborne Rd	17 B2
Windmill Rd	17 B3

BOURNEMOUTH
BOSCOMBE

Adeline Rd	19 D2
Albermarle Rd	18 A1
Albert Rd	18 A3
Alford Rd	18 A1
Allington Rd	18 B1
Alma Rd	18 B1
Alyth Rd	18 A1
Annerley Rd	19 C2
Arcadia Av	18 B1
Argyll Rd	19 D2
Arthur Clo	18 B2
Ascham Rd	19 C2
Ashley Rd	19 D1
Austin Clo	19 C2
Avenue La	18 A3
Avenue Rd	18 A3
Avon Clo	19 C1
Avon Rd	19 C1
Aylesbury Rd	19 D2
Bath Rd	18 B3
Beacon Rd	18 A3
Beechey Rd	18 B2
Beechwood Av	19 D2
Beechwood Gdns	19 D2
Belvedere Rd	18 B1
Bennett Rd	19 C1
Berkeley Rd	18 A1
Berwick Rd	19 C1
Bethia Clo	19 C1
Bethia Rd	19 C1
Bingham Rd	18 B1
Bodorgan Rd	18 A2
Bonham Rd	18 A1
Borthwick Rd	19 D2
Boscombe Cliff Rd	19 D3
Boscombe Grove Rd	19 C2
Boscombe Overcliff	
Dri	19 D3
Boscombe Prom	19 D3
Boscombe Spa Rd	19 C2
Bourne Av	18 A3
Bradburne Rd	18 A3
Braidley Rd	18 A2
Branksome Wood Gdns	18 A2
Branksome Wood Rd	18 A2
Browning Av	19 D2
Bryanstone Rd	18 A1
Buchanan Av	19 D1
Byron Rd	19 D3
Cambridge Rd	18 A3
Campbell Rd	19 D2
Capstone Pl	19 C1
Capstone Rd	18 B1
Carlton Rd	19 C2
Carnarvon Rd	19 D2
Carysfort Rd	19 C2
Cavendish Clo	18 B2
Cavendish Rd	18 B2
Cawdor Rd	18 A1
Cecil Av	19 C1
Cecil Rd	19 D2
Central Dri, Boscombe	19 D1
Central Dri,	
Bournemouth	18 A2
Charminster Rd	18 B1
Chatworth Rd	18 B1
Chessel Av	19 D2
Chine Cres	18 A3
Chine Cres Rd	18 A3
Christchurch Rd	18 B3
Churchill Rd	19 D2
Cleveland Gdns	19 C2
Cleveland Rd	19 C2
Commercial Rd	18 A3

Corporation Rd	19 C2
Cotlands Rd	18 B2
Crabton Close Rd	19 D2
Cranborne Rd	18 A3
Crescent Rd	18 A3
Crimea Rd	18 A1
Cromer Rd	19 C1
Cumnor Rd	18 B3
Curzon Rd	19 C1
Cyril Rd	19 C1
De Lisle Rd	18 A1
Dean Park Cres	18 B2
Dean Park Rd	18 B2
Derby Rd	19 C2
Donoughmore Rd	19 D2
Drummond Rd	19 C2
Dunbar Rd	18 A1
Dunkeld Rd	18 A1
Durley Chine	18 A3
Durley Chine Rd	18 A3
Durley Chine Rd Sth	18 A3
Durley Gdns	18 A3
Durley Rd	18 A3
Durran Rd	18 A2
East Av	18 A1
East Cliff Prom	18 B3
East Overcliff Dri	18 B3
Egerton Gdns	19 C1
Egerton Rd	19 C1
Elgin Rd	18 A1
Elwyn Rd	19 C2
Exeter Cres	18 A3
Exeter La	18 A3
Exeter Park Rd	18 A3
Exeter Rd	18 A3
Fir Vale Rd	18 B3
Fitzharris Av	18 B1
Florence Rd	19 D2
Fortescue Rd	18 B1
Frances Rd	19 C2
Gainsborough Rd	19 D1
Garfield Av	19 C2
Gerald Rd	18 B1
Gervis Pl	18 A3
Gervis Rd	18 B3
Gilbert Rd	19 C1
Gladstone Rd	19 D2
Glen Fern Rd	18 B3
Glen Rd	19 D2
Glencoe Rd	19 D1
Glenferness Av	18 A1
Gloucester Rd	19 D2
Gordon Rd	19 C2
Grafton Rd	18 B1
Grantham Rd	19 D2
Grantley Rd	19 D2
Grants Av	19 C1
Grants Clo	19 D1
Grasmere Rd	19 D2
Grosvenor Gdns	19 D2
Grove Rd	18 B3
Grovely Av	19 D3
Hamilton Clo	19 C2
Hamilton Rd	19 C2
Hannemann Rd	18 C3
Harewood Av	19 D1
Harewood Cres	19 D1
Harrison Av	19 C1
Haviland Mews	19 D2
Haviland Rd	19 D2
Haviland Rd W	19 D2
Hawkwood Rd	19 D2
Hayes Rd	19 D1
Heathcote Rd	19 D2
Hengist Rd	19 C2
Henville Rd	19 C2
Heron Court Rd	18 B1
Hinton Rd	18 B3
Holdenhurst Rd	19 B2
Horace Rd	19 D2
Howard Rd	19 C1
Huntly Rd	18 A1
Ibsley Clo	19 C1
Iddlesleigh Rd	18 B1
Jefferson Av	19 C1
Kensington Dri	18 A2
Kerley Rd	18 A3
Keswick Rd	19 D2
Kings Park	19 D1
Kings Park Dri	19 D1
Kings Park Rd	19 D1
Kings Rd	18 B1
Kinross Rd	18 A1
Knole Gdns	19 C2
Knole Rd	19 C2
Knyveton Rd	19 C2
Langton Rd	19 D2
Lansdowne Cres	18 B3

Lansdowne Gdns	18 B2
Lansdowne Rd	18 B2
Leamington Rd	18 B1
Leeson Rd	19 D1
Leven Av	18 A2
Lincoln Av	19 C1
Linwood Rd	18 B1
Little Forest Rd	18 A2
Littledown Av	19 D1
Littledown Rd	19 D1
Lonsdale Rd	18 A1
Lorne Park Rd	18 B3
Lowther Gdns	19 C2
Lowther Rd	18 B1
Lytton Rd	19 C2
Madeira Rd	18 B2
Madison Av	19 C1
Malmesbury Park	18 B1
Malmesbury Park Pl	19 C2
Malmesbury Park Rd	18 B1
Manor Rd	18 C3
Marina Clo	19 D3
Maxwell Rd	18 B1
Merlewood Clo	18 A2
Methuen Clo	19 C2
Methuen Rd	18 B2
Meyrick Park Cres	18 A1
Meyrick Rd	18 B3
Michelgrove Rd	19 D3
Milton Rd	18 A2
Moorland Rd	19 C2
Mount Stuart Rd	19 D3
Myrtle Rd	19 C1
Nairn Rd	18 A1
North Rd	19 D2
Northcote Rd	19 C2
Nortoft Rd	18 B1
Norwich Av West	18 A3
Norwich Rd	18 A3
Oak Rd	19 C1
Oban Rd	18 A1
Old Christchurch Rd	18 A3
Ophir Gdns	19 C2
Ophir Rd	18 B2
Orchard St	18 A3
Orcheston Rd	19 C1
Overcliff Dri	18 A3
Owls Rd	19 D3
Oxford Rd	18 B2
Palmerston Rd	19 D2
Park Rd	18 B2
Parker Rd	18 A1
Parsonage Rd	18 B3
Percy Rd	19 D2
Pier Approach	18 B3
Poole Hill	18 A3
Poole Rd	18 A3
Portchester Pl	18 B2
Portchester Rd	18 B1
Portman Rd	19 D2
Post Office Rd	18 A3
Priory Rd	18 A3
Purbeck Rd	18 A3
Queens Gdns	18 A2
Queens Park Gdns	19 C1
Queens Park Rd	19 C1
Queens Park S Dri	19 C1
Queens Park W Dri	19 C1
Randolph Rd	19 D2
Richmond Bridge Rd	19 C1
Richmond Gdns	18 B2
Richmond Hill	18 A3
Richmond Hill Dri	18 A2
Richmond Park Av	18 B1
Richmond Park Cres	18 C1
Richmond Park Rd	19 C1
Richmond Wood Rd	18 B1
Roslin Rd	18 A1
Roumelia La	19 D2
Royal Arcade	18 B3
Rushton Cres	18 A1
Russell Cotes Rd	18 B3
St Albans Av	18 B1
St Albans Cres	18 B1
St Anthonys Rd	18 A2
St Augustins Rd	18 A1
St Clements Gdns	19 C2
St Clements Rd	19 C2
St Ives Gdns	18 B2
St Johns Rd	19 D2
St Ledgers Pl	19 C1
St Ledgers Rd	19 C1
St Leonards Rd	18 B1
St Lukes Rd	18 A1
St Marys Rd	19 C1
St Michaels Rd	18 A3
St Pauls La	18 B2
St Pauls Rd	18 B2

St Peters Rd 18 B3
St Stephens Rd 18 A2
St Swithuns 18 B2
St Valerie Rd 18 A2
St Winifreds Rd 18 A2
Salisbury Rd 19 D2
Sea Rd 19 D3
Shaftesbury Rd 19 C1
Shelbourne Rd 18 B1
Shelley Rd 19 D2
Silchester Clo 18 A2
Soberton Dri 19 C1
Somerset Rd 19 D2
Somerville Rd 18 A3
South Rd, Boscombe 19 D2
South Rd,
  Bournemouth 18 B3
South Roslin Rd 18 A1
Southcote Rd 19 C2
Southview Pl 18 A3
Spencer Rd 19 C2
Spring Rd 19 C2
Stafford Rd 18 B2
Stanley Rd 19 C2
Stewart Clo 19 C2
Stewart Rd 18 B1
Stirling Rd 18 A1
Stoke Wood Rd 18 B1
Stour Rd 19 C1
Suffolk Rd 18 A3
Summerfields 19 D1
Surrey Rd 18 A2
Talbot Av 18 A1
Talbot Rd 18 A1
Tamworth Rd 19 D2
Terrace Mt 18 A3
Terrace Rd 18 A3
The Arcade 18 A3
The Crescent 19 D2
The Marina 19 D3
The Square 18 A3
The Triangle 18 A3
Thistlebarrow Rd 19 D1
Tower Rd 19 D2
Trafalgar Rd 18 B1
Tregonwell Rd 18 A3
Trinity Rd 18 B2
Truscott Av 18 B1
Undercliff Dri 18 B3
Undercliff Rd 19 D3
Upper Hinton Rd 18 B3
Upper Norwich Rd 18 A3
Upper Terrace Rd 18 A3
Vale Rd 19 C2
Verulam Pl 18 A3
Victoria Pl 19 C2
Victoria Rd 19 C2
Walpole Rd 19 C2
Washington Av 19 C1
Waterloo Rd 18 A1
Watkin Rd 19 D2
Waverley Rd 18 B2
Wellington Rd 18 B1
Wessex Way 18 A2
West Cliff Gdns 18 A3
West Cliff Prom 18 A3
West Cliff Rd 18 A3
West Undercliff Prom 18 A3
Westby Rd 19 D2
Westhill Pl 18 A3
Westhill Rd 18 A3
Weston Dri 18 B3
Westover Rd 18 B3
Wharncliffe Rd 19 C2
Wilfred Rd 19 D2
William Rd 19 D1
Wilson Rd 19 C2
Wilton Rd 19 D2
Wimborne Rd 18 A2
Windermere Rd 18 B1
Windham Rd 19 C2
Windsor Rd 19 D2
Wollstonecraft Rd 19 D3
Wolverton Rd 19 D2
Woodford Rd 19 C2
Wootton Gdns 18 B3
Wootton Mt 18 B3
Wychwood Dri 18 A2
Yelverton Rd 18 A3
York Pl 19 D2
York Rd 18 B2

BOVINGTON CAMP

Alamein Rd 22 B4
Amiens Rd 22 A3
Andover Grn 22 A4
Arras Rd 22 A3
Balaclava Rd 22 A3
Bony Rd 22 B3
Bovington La 22 A4
Cachy Rd 22 A3
Capper Rd 22 A3
Cologne Rd 22 B3
Cranesmoor Clo 22 A3
Cunningham Clo 22 B3
Duncan Cres 22 B4
8th August Rd 22 A3
Elles Rd 22 A3
Erin Rd 22 A3
Foxbury 22 A3
Framerville Rd 22 A3
Gaza Rd 22 A3
Heath Clo 22 A3
Higher Wood 22 A4
Holt Rd 22 A3
King George V Rd 22 A3
Linsay Rd 22 A4
Morris Rd 22 B4
New Rd 22 A3
Rhine Rd 22 A3
Robertson Rd 22 A3
St Julien Rd 22 A3
Sewell Rd 22 A3
Sir Richard Hull Rd 22 A3
Swinton Av 22 A3
Wain Rd 22 A2

BRIDPORT BOTHENHAMPTON

Acre Av 20 C1
Alexandra Rd 20 A2
Allington Gdns 20 A1
Allington Pk 20 A2
Armstrong Rd 20 B1
Arrowfield 20 A2
Asker Gdns 20 B2
Asker Mead 20 B2
Banton Shard 20 C1
Barrack St 20 B2
Beaminster Rd 20 C1
Beaumont Av 20 C2
Bedford Pl 20 B2
Bothen Dri 20 B2
Bowhayes 21 B3
Bramley Hill 20 C1
Brit View Rd 21 A4
Broad La 21 A3
Broadmead Av 20 A2
Burton Rd 21 B3
Caley Way 20 C1
Chard Mead Rd 20 B2
Cherrytree La 20 A1
Cherrytrees 20 A1
Chestnut Rd 21 B3
Church St 20 B2
Claremont Gdns 20 B1
Claremont Rd 20 B1
Coneygar Clo 20 B1
Coneygar La 20 B1
Coopers Dri 21 B3
Coronation Rd 20 A2
Court Clo 20 C1
Court Orchard Rd 20 A1
Crock La 21 B3
Dark La 21 A3
Delapre 20 B2
Diments Sq 20 A1
Dodhams La 20 B1
Donkey La 20 A1
Dottery Rd 20 A1
Downes St 20 B2
Drew Clo 20 C1
Duck St 21 B3
East Rd 20 B2
East St 20 B2
Edgehill Rd 21 A3
Elizabeth Av 21 A3
Elwell 21 B3
Esplanade 21 A4
First Cliff Walk 21 A4
Fishweir Flds 20 C1
Fishweir La 20 C1
Flaxhayes 20 B3
Flood La 21 B3
Folly Mill 20 B2
Folly Mill Gdns 20 B2
Folly Mill La 20 B2
Forsters La 20 C1
Foundry La 20 A2
Fourth Cliff Walk 21 A4
Fox Clo 20 C1
Fulbrooks Clo 20 A2
Fulbrooks La 20 A2
Gale Cres 20 A2
George St 21 B4
Gladstone Clo 20 C2
Glebe Clo 21 B3
Glebelands 20 B2
Gore Cross Way 20 C1
Gore La 20 C1
Green Clo 20 C1
Green La, Walditch 20 C2
Green La,
  Bothenhampton 21 B3
Grove Pymore Rd 20 B1
Gundry La 20 B2
Gypsy La 20 B1
Happy Island Way 20 C2
Hardy Rd 20 B2
Hibernia Pl 20 A1
Higher Pymore 20 B1
Higher St 20 C1
Hill Clo 21 A4
Hillingdon 20 C1
Hillview, Bradpole 20 C1
Hillview,
  Court Orchard 20 A1
Hollow Way 21 B3
Hospital La 20 A1
Jessops Av 20 C2
Journeys End 20 A2
Katherines Dri 20 C1
Kenwyn Rd 20 B2
King Charles Way 20 C2
King St 20 B2
King William Head 20 C1
Kings Head 20 C1
Kingsnorth Clo 20 C2
Knightstone Rise 20 C1
Lake La 21 B3
Lansdowne Rd 21 B3
Laurel Clo 20 A1
Lee La 20 C2
Long La, Bridport 20 B2
Long La,
  Bothenhampton 21 B3
Lower Walditch La 20 C2
Magdalane La 20 A2
Main St 21 B3
Manor Fields 20 C2
Maple Gdns 21 B3
Marrowbone La 21 C3
Marsh Barn Rd 21 B4
Marsh Gate 21 B3
Mead Flds 20 A1
Mead La 20 A1
Meadow Ct 20 B2
Meadway 21 A4
Meech Clo 21 B3
Middle St 20 C1
Mount Pleasant 20 A2
Mountjoy 21 B3
Nordons 21 B3
Norman Clo 20 C2
Normandy Way 20 B2
North Allington 20 A1
North Hill Way 21 B3
North Mills Rd 20 B2
North St 20 B2
Nursery Gdns 20 B2
Old Church Rd 21 B3
Orchard Av 20 B1
Orchard Cres 20 A1
Osbourne Rd 20 B2
Pageants Clo 20 C1
Park Rd 20 A2
Parsonage Rd 20 A1
Pasture Way 21 B3
Pier Ter 21 A4
Pine Vw 20 A2
Princess Rd 21 A3
Priory La 20 B2
Pymore 20 B1
Pymore Ter 21 A4
Quarry La 21 B3
Quayside 21 A4
Queens Av 20 A2
Rax La 20 B2
Ridgeway 20 C1
Rope Walk 20 B2
Ropes Ct 20 B2
Roundham Gdns 21 B3
St Andrews Cres 20 B2
St Andrews Gdns 20 C1
St Andrews Rd 20 B2
St Katherines Av 20 B2
St Lukes Ct 20 A1
St Michaels La 20 A2
St Swithins Av 20 A2
St Swithins Rd 20
Sea Road Nth 20
Sea Road Sth 21
Seaward Gdns 21
Second Cliff Walk 21
Shoe La 20
Simene Clo 20
Skilling Hill Rd 21
Slades Green 21
South Lawns 21
South Mill La 21
South Rd 21
South St 20
South Walk 20
Sparacre Gdns 20
Spring Clo 20
Station Rd 21
Stuart Way 20
Tannery Rd 20
Third Cliff Walk 21
Trinity Way 20
Trustin Clo 20
Uplands 20
Valley Rd 21
Vearse Clo 21
Victoria Gro 20
Village Rd 20
Walditch Rd 20
Wander Well 21
Warne Hill 20
Watton Gdns 20
Watton La 21
Watton Park 21
Wellfield Rd 20
West Allington 20
West Bay Rd 21
West Cliff 21
West Rd 20
West St 20
West Walk 21
White Clo 20
Willow Way 20
Wych Hill 21
Wych Ridge 21

BROADMAYNE WEST KNIGHTON

Bakers Paddock 15
Beech Clo 15
Bramble Drove 15
Bramble Edge 15
Broadmead 15
Chalky Rd 15
Charlmont Cross 15
Conway Dri 15
Cowleaze Rd 15
Cross Trees Clo 15
Glebe Way 15
High Trees 15
Knighton La 15
Lewell Way 15
Main St 15
Martel Clo 15
Osmington Drove 15
Rectory Clo 15
Rectory Rd 15
St Martins Clo 15
South Vw 15
Spring Gdns 15
Stafford Clo 15
The Spinney 15
Watergates La 15
Woodlands 15

BURTON BRADSTOCK

Annings La 22
Barr La 22
Beach Rd 22
Bindbarrow Rd 22
Bredy Rd 22
Burton Rd 22
Chapel St 22
Charles Rd 22
Church St 22
Cliff Rd 22
Common La 22
Darby La 22
Grove Orchard 22
Grove Rd 22
High St 22
Hive Clo 22
Lower Townsend 22
Mill St 22

Norburton 22 B1
Shadrach 22 A1
Shipton La 22 A1
South Annings 22 A1
Southover 22 A2

CHARMINSTER

Broken Cross 23 B2
Burn Vw 23 B2
Charlotte Clo 23 B2
Cocklands 23 B2
Down End 23 B1
East Hill 23 B2
Ellerslie Clo 23 B1
Gascoyne La 23 A2
Green Acre 23 B2
Highfield Clo 23 A1
Hill Vw 23 A2
Meadow View 23 A4
Mill La 23 B1
North St 23 A1
Pound Clo 23 A2
Sodern La 23 A1
Symonds Ct 23 B2
The Square 23 A2
Vicarage Gdns 23 B2
Vicarage La 23 B2
Wanchard La 23 A1
Weir View 23 A1
West Hill 23 B2
Westleaze 23 B2
Westleaze Clo 23 B2
York Clo 23 B2

CHARMOUTH

Axminster Rd 23 A3
Bridge Rd 23 B3
Charberry Rise 23 A3
Downside Clo 23 A3
Ellesdon 23 B3
Five Acres 23 A3
Gardenside 23 A3
Greenhayes 23 A3
Higher Sea La 23 A3
Kidmore Clo 23 A3
Lower Sea La 23 B4
Old Lyme Hill 23 A3
OLd Lyme La 23 A3
Orchard Clo 23 A3
River Way 23 B4
St Andrews Dri 23 A3
The Street 23 A3
Wesley Clo 23 B3
Westcliffe Rd 23 A3

CHICKERELL

Aldabrand Clo 24 A2
Browns Cres 24 B2
Chickerell Hill 24 A1
Chickerell Rd 24 A2
Coldharbour 24 B1
East St 24 A2
Elziver Clo 24 A2
Fairfield 24 A2
Fishermans Clo 24 B2
Fleet La 24 A2
Fleet Rd 24 A2
Garston Hill 24 A2
Glennie Way 24 B2
Green La 24 B2
Higher End 24 A2
Lerrett Clo 24 B2
Lower Putton La 24 B2
Lower Way 24 A2
Mariners Way 24 B2
Marshallsay Rd 24 A1
Meadow Clo 24 A2
North Sq 24 A2
Putton La 24 B2
Randall Clo 24 A2
Rashley Rd 24 A2
Rex La 24 A2
School Clo 24 B2
School Hill 24 B1
Spiller Rd 24 A2
West Clo 24 A2
West St 24 A2
Whynot Way 24 A2
Wilmslow Rd 24 A1

CHRISTCHURCH

Addington Pl 27 C2
Addiscombe Rd 26 A2

Airfield Rd 27 D2
Airfield Way 27 D2
Albion Rd 26 A1
Alder Clo 27 C1
Alexander Clo 27 C2
Ambassador Clo 27 D2
Ambury La 27 C1
Amethyst Rd 27 C2
Amsterdam Sq 26 B2
Anchor Clo 27 D3
Anne Clo 26 A1
Anson Clo 27 D2
Arcadia Rd 26 A1
Argle Rd 27 C3
Ariel Clo 26 B3
Ariel Dri 26 B3
Arthur La 26 A2
Arthur Rd 26 A2
Athelstan Rd 26 A3
Auster Clo 27 D2
Avenue Rd 26 A2
Avon Bldgs 26 B2
Avon Rd E 26 A1
Avon Rd W 26 A1
Avon Wharf 26 B2
Baldwin Clo 27 C2
Bank Clo 26 B2
Bargates 26 B2
Baring Rd 26 A3
Barrack Rd 26 A1
Beaconsfield Rd 26 B2
Beaulieu Av 26 A2
Beaulieu Rd 26 A2
Belfield Rd 26 A3
Belle Vue Cres 26 A3
Belle Vue Rd 26 A3
Belvedere Rd 26 A2
Beresford Gdns 27 C2
Bingham Clo 27 C2
Bingham Rd 27 C2
Blackberry La 27 C2
Blenheim Dri 27 D2
Bodowen Clo 27 C1
Bodowen Rd 27 C1
Bonnington Clo 27 C1
Brabazon Dri 27 D2
Braemar Av 26 A3
Braemar Clo 26 A3
Branders Clo 26 A3
Branders La 26 B3
Branwell Clo 26 A1
Briar Clo 27 C2
Bridge St 26 B2
Brightlands Av 26 A3
Brittania Way 27 D2
Broadlands Av 26 A3
Broadway 26 A3
Bronte Av 26 A1
Bub La 27 C2
Buccaneers Clo 27 C2
Bure Haven Dri 27 D2
Bure Homage Gdns 27 D2
Bure Homage La 27 D2
Bure La 27 D3
Burnett Rd 26 A2
Burton Rd 27 C2
Calton Av 26 A2
Cameron Rd 27 C2
Campion Gro 27 D2
Carbery Av 26 A3
Caroline Av 27 C2
Castle St 26 B2
Cataline Clo 27 D2
Caxton Clo 27 D2
Charles Rd 27 D1
Charlotte Clo 27 D2
Christchurch By-Pass 26 B2
Church La 26 B2
Church St 26 B2
Clarendon Rd 26 A2
Coast Guard Way 27 C3
Coleridge Grn 27 D1
Comet Way 27 D2
Court Clo 27 C2
Cranleigh Clo 26 A3
Cranleigh Rd 26 A3
Creedy Path 26 B2
Cricket Clo 27 D3
Cringle Av 26 A3
Croft Rd 27 D2
Crofton Clo 26 A1
Cunningham Clo 27 D2
Curlew Rd 27 D2
Danesbury Av 26 A3
Darwin Av 26 A1
De Haviland Way 27 D3
Delft Mews 27 C1
Delta Clo 27 D2

Dennistoun Av 27 C2
Devon Rd 26 A1
Disraeii Rd 27 C2
Donnelly Rd 26 A3
Dorset Rd 27 C1
Douglas Av 26 A2
Douglas Rd 26 A3
Drake Clo 27 D2
Draper Rd 27 C2
Druitt Rd 27 C1
Duncliff Rd 26 A3
Dunlin Clo 27 D3
Edward Rd 27 D1
Elderberry La 27 D2
Elizabeth Av 26 A1
Emily Clo 26 A1
Endfield Clo 26 A1
Endfield Rd 26 A1
Everest Rd 27 C1
Fairfield 26 B2
Fairmile Rd 26 A1
Fairway Dri 26 A2
Falcon Dri 27 D3
Fisherman's Bank 27 C3
Fitzmaurice Rd 26 A1
Flambard Av 26 A1
Foxholes Rd 26 A3
Foxwood Av 27 C3
Freda Rd 26 A2
Frobisher Clo 27 D2
Fulmar Rd 27 D3
Gladstone Clo 27 C2
Gleadowe Av 26 A2
Glendale Rd 26 A3
Gordon Way 26 B1
Grafton Clo 27 C2
Grange Rd 27 D2
Grebe Clo 27 D2
Green Acres 27 D2
Grove Rd E 26 A1
Grove Rd W 26 A1
Groveley Rd 27 C2
Haarlem Mews 27 C2
Halewood Way 26 A1
Halifax Way 27 D2
Harbour Cres 27 C3
Harbour Rd 26 B3
Hardy Clo 27 D3
Harland Rd 26 A3
Hawkins Clo 27 D2
Hawthorn Clo 26 A1
Hawthorn Rd 27 C1
High St 26 B2
Highcliffe Rd 27 D1
Hill Rd 26 A3
Hillary Rd 27 C1
Holly Gdns 27 C1
Homelands 26 A2
Honeybourne Cres 26 A3
Horsa Rd 26 A3
Howard Clo 27 D2
Howe Clo 27 D3
Hunt Rd 27 C1
Hunter Clo 27 D2
Iford Clo 26 A2
Iford La 26 A2
Inveravon 27 D3
Irvine Way 27 C1
Jellicoe Dri 27 D2
Johnston Rd 27 C2
Jumpers Rd 26 A1
Kestrel Dri 27 D2
Keyes Clo 27 D2
Kimberley Clo 26 A1
Kings Av 26 A2
Kingsley Av 26 A3
Kingsley Clo 26 A3
Knapp Clo 26 A1
Lark Rd 27 D2
Latch Farm Av 26 A1
Latchmill Clo 26 A1
Ledbury Rd 27 C3
Leyside 27 D2
Lineside 26 B1
Lingwood Av 27 C2
Livingstone Rd 27 C2
Lyndhurst Rd 27 D1
Magdalen La 26 A2
Magnolia Clo 26 A3
Mallard Way 27 D2
Mallory Clo 27 D1
Manor Rd 26 A2
Marmion Grn 27 C2
Marsh Ditch 26 A2
Marsh La 27 C2
Martins Hill Clo 26 B1
Martins Hill La 26 B1
Meadowland 27 C2

Medlar Clo 27 C1
Melbourne Rd 26 A1
Merlin Way 27 D3
Mill Rd 26 A1
Millhams St 26 B2
Minterne Rd 27 C3
Moffat Rd 27 C2
Monksnell Grn 27 C2
Mortimer Clo 27 D2
Mountbatten Clo 27 D3
Mude Gdns 27 D3
Mudeford Grn Clo 27 D3
Mudeford La 27 C2
Mudeford 27 D3
Nelson Dri 27 D2
Newcombe Rd 26 A2
Newlands Rd 27 D2
Normanton Clo 26 A1
Nugent Rd 27 C2
Old Priory Rd 26 A3
Orchard St 26 A2
Orchid Way 26 B2
Palmerston Av 27 C2
Park Gdns 27 C2
Pauntley Rd 27 C2
Pelham Clo 27 C2
Peregrine Rd 27 D2
Pinehurst Av 27 D3
Pipers Dri 27 D2
Portfield Clo 26 A1
Portfield Rd 26 A2
Princess Av 26 B2
Priory Ct 26 B2
Priory Quay 26 B3
Purewell 27 C2
Quay Rd 26 B2
Queens Av 26 B3
Queens Rd 27 C2
Raleigh Clo 27 D3
Raven Way 27 D3
Redvers Rd 27 C2
Ricardo Cres 27 D2
Riverlea Rd 26 A2
Riversdale Rd 26 A3
Riverside La 26 A3
Riverside Rd 26 A3
Robins Way 27 D3
Rodney Dri 27 D2
Rolls Dri 26 B3
Roscrea Clo 26 B3
Roscrea Dri 26 B3
Rosedale Clo 27 C2
Rotterdam Dri 27 C2
Rowena Rd 26 A3
Rushford Warren 27 D3
Russell Dri 27 C2
Rutland Rd 26 A1
St Catherines Rd 26 A3
St Johns Rd 26 A2
St Margarets Av 26 B2
Salisbury Rd 27 C1
Sandown Rd 26 B1
Sandy Plot 26 A2
Saxonbury Rd 27 D1
Scotts Grn 27 C2
Scotts Hill La 27 C2
Sheldrake Rd 27 D3
Sherwood Clo 26 A2
Shorts Clo 26 B1
Silver St 26 B2
Slinn Rd 27 C2
Somerford Av 27 D1
Somerford Rd 27 C2
Somerford Way 27 C2
Sopers La 26 B3
Sorrell Way 27 D1
South View Rd 26 A2
Southey Rd 27 D1
Southlands Av 26 A3
Southlea Av 26 A3
Springfield Av 26 A3
Stanpit 27 C2
Station Rd 26 A2
Stirling Way 27 D2
Stony La 26 B1
Stony La Sth 26 B2
Stour Rd 26 A3
Stoursbank Rd 26 A2
Stroud Gdns 27 C2
Stroud La 27 C2
Stroud Park Av 27 C2
Summers La 27 C1
Sunnylands Av 26 A3
Swordfish Dri 27 D2
Sydney Rd 26 A1
Tensing Rd 27 C1
The Coppice 27 D2
The Hawthorns 27 C2

Thornbury Rd 26 A3
Tilburg Rd 26 B2
Treebys Clo 27 C1
Tuckton Rd 26 A3
Twynham Av 26 A2
Twynham Rd 26 A3
Utrecht Ct 27 C2
Verwood Cres 26 B3
Victoria Rd 27 C3
Viking Clo 26 A3
Viking Way 26 A3
Villette Clo 26 A1
Viscount Dri 27 D2
Walcott Av 26 A1
Warren Av 27 D3
Watermill Rd 26 A1
Waterside 27 D3
Watery La 27 D1
Wayside Rd 26 A3
Westfield Rd 26 A3
Westview Rd 27 C2
Whitehall 26 B2
Whitehayes Rd 26 B1
Wick La, Christchurch 26 B2
Wick La, Wick 26 B3
Wickfield Av 26 B2
Wickfield Clo 26 B2
Wickneads Rd 26 A3
Wicklea Rd 26 B3
Wildfell Clo 26 A1
Wildown Rd 26 A3
Willow Dri 26 A3
Willow Way 26 A3
Wilverly Rd 27 D2
Wren Clo 27 D3
York Clo 26 A2

CORFE CASTLE

Battlemead 24 B4
Calcraft Rd 24 B4
Colletts Clo 24 B4
East St 24 A3
Halves Cotts 24 A4
Higher Filbank 24 B4
Higher Gdns 24 B4
Market Sq 24 A3
Mead Rd 24 B4
Sandy Hill La 24 A3
Springwell Clo 24 B4
Tilbury Mead 24 B4
Townsend Rd 24 A4
Webbers Clo 24 A4
West St 24 A3

CORFE MULLEN

Abbotsbury Rd 25 C1
Albert Rd 25 B1
Amber Rd 25 A2
Anvil Cres 25 C1
Ascot Rd 25 C2
Barry Gdns 25 C1
Barters La 25 C2
Beacon Rd 25 B2
Beacon Way 25 B2
Beech Clo 25 B2
Birch Clo 25 B1
Blacksmith Clo 25 B1
Blaney Way 25 B1
Blythe Rd 25 B1
Bognor Rd 25 C2
Broadmoor Rd 25 A1
Broadstone Way 25 A1
Brook La 25 A1
Brownsea Av 25 B1
Caesars Way 25 B2
Cecil Clo 25 B1
Central Av 25 B1
Chapel Clo 25 B1
Chapel La 25 A1
Cheam Rd 25 C2
Clarendon Rd 25 C2
Colin Clo 25 B2
Corfe Gdns 25 B2
Corfe Lodge Rd 25 B2
Corfe View Rd 25 B1
Corfe Way 25 C2
Cotton Clo 25 C1
Coventry Clo 25 A2
Croft Clo 25 B1
Dalkeith Rd 25 B1
Dell Clo 25 C2
Dennis Rd 25 B1
East Way 25 B1
Erica Dri 25 B1
Firside Rd 25 B2

Gladelands Clo 25 B2
Gladelands Way 25 B2
Gorse Rd 25 A1
Gurney Rd 25 B1
Hadley Way 25 B2
Hamilton Rd 25 B1
Hanham Rd 25 B1
Haven Rd 25 B1
Heather Clo 25 C1
Heckford Rd 25 B1
Henbury Clo 25 B1
Henbury Rise 25 B1
Henbury View Rd 25 B1
High Park Rd 25 C2
High Way 25 C2
Higher Blandford Rd 25 C1
Highfield Clo 25 B1
Highfield Rd 25 B2
Highmoor Clo 25 B1
Highmoor Rd 25 B1
Hillcrest Rd 25 B1
Hillside Gdns 25 A2
Hillside Rd 25 A2
Hilltop Rd 25 B1
Holland Way 25 C1
Insley Cres 25 B1
Ivor Rd 25 B2
Jubilee Rd 25 B1
Kiln Clo 25 A2
Knoll La 25 A1
Lancaster Clo 25 C1
Lancaster Dri 25 C1
Laurel Clo 25 B1
Lavender Way 25 B2
Lewesdon Dri 25 C2
Link Rise 25 B1
Lytchett Dri 25 C2
Marian Clo 25 A2
Marian Rd 25 A2
Maxwell Rd 25 B2
Meadow Rise 25 C1
Moorside Rd 25 B1
Newlands Way 25 B2
Northbrook Rd 25 C2
Phillips Rd 25 B1
Primrose Way 25 B1
Pye Clo 25 B1
Queens Rd 25 B1
Roman Rd 25 B2
Rushall La 25 A1
Rushcombe Way 25 B1
Sandford Way 25 C2
Silverdale Clo 25 C2
South Rd 25 B1
Southlands Av 25 B1
Springdale Av 25 C1
Springdale Gro 25 B2
Springdale Rd 25 B2
Sutherland Av 25 C1
Tadden Walk 25 C2
Terence Rd 25 B1
The Close 25 B2
Upton Way 25 C2
Victoria Clo 25 B2
Viewside Clo 25 B1
Wareham Rd 25 A2
Waterloo Rd 25 A1
Wayman Rd 25 C1
West Way 25 C2
Wickham Dri 25 B2
Widworthy Dri 25 C1
Wills Clo 25 B2
Wyatts Clo 25 B1
Wyatts La 25 B1
Wynne Clo 25 C2
York Rd 25 C2

CROSSWAYS

Airfield Clo 46 A4
Binghams Rd 46 A3
Briars End 46 B3
Combe Way 46 A4
Dick O th Banks Clo 46 B3
Dick O th Banks Rd 46 A3
Egdon La 46 B3
Empool Clo 46 A4
Green La 46 B3
Grey Stones Clo 46 B3
Heathland Clo 46 A4
Hope Clo 46 B4
Hurricane Clo 46 A3
Moreton Rd 46 B3
Mount Skippet Way 46 A4
Moynton Clo 46 A3
Old Farm Way 46 B4
Redbridge Rd 46 B3

Spitfire Clo 46 A4
Station Rd 46 B3
Warmwell Rd 46 A4
West Link Rd 46 A3

DORCHESTER

Ackerman Rd 29 C2
Acland Rd 28 B2
Albert Rd 28 B2
Alexandra Rd 28 B2
Alexandra Ter 28 B2
Alfred Pl 29 C2
Alfred Rd 28 B2
Alice Rd 28 A2
Alington Ter 29 C1
All Saints Rd 29 C2
Allington Av 29 C2
Allington St 28 B1
Apollo Clo 28 A3
Arbutus Clo 28 B2
Arnhem Grn 28 A1
Ashley Rd 28 B2
Athelstan Rd 29 C2
Augustin Clo 28 A3
Balmoral Cres 29 C3
Barnes Way 29 C2
Barrow Clo 28 A3
Baynards Rd 28 A2
Beech Ct 28 B2
Blagdon Rd 28 A2
Bockhampton Rd 29 D1
Bowling Alley Walk 28 B2
Braemar Rd 29 C2
Bridport Rd 28 A2
Britannia Way 28 A3
Buckingham Way 29 C3
Caernarvon Clo 29 C3
Caesar Grn 28 A2
Cambridge Rd 28 A2
Camden Way 28 A3
Came View Clo 29 D2
Came View Rd 29 D2
Capitol Clo 28 A3
Casterbridge Rd 29 D2
Castle Clo 28 A2
Caters Pl 28 B1
Cedar Rd 28 A1
Celtic Cres 28 A3
Charles St 28 B2
Chestnut Way 28 A1
Church Acre 29 C2
Church Clo 28 B1
Church St 28 B1
Clarence Rd 28 A3
Claudius Clo 28 A3
Coburg Rd 28 A2
Colliton St 28 B1
Conway Walk 29 C3
Corn Hill 28 B1
Cornwall Rd 28 B2
Cromwell Rd 28 B2
Culliford Rd Nth 29 C2
Culliford Rd Sth 29 C2
Cunnington Clo 28 A3
Dagmar Rd 28 B2
Damers Rd 28 A2
Diana Clo 28 B3
Druids Walk 28 B3
Dukes Av 29 C2
Durngate St 28 B1
Durnover Ct 29 C1
Earl Clo 29 C2
Eddison Av 29 C2
Edward Rd 28 B2
Egdon Clo 29 C3
Elizabeth Pl 28 A2
Fairfield Rd 28 B2
Farringdon Clo 28 B3
Fenway Clo 29 D2
Firtree Clo 28 A1
Florence Rd 28 A3
Fordington 29 C2
Fordington Gdns 28 B1
Fortress Grn 28 A3
Forum Grn 28 A3
Fosse Grn 28 A3
Fourgates Rd 28 A2
Friars Clo 29 C2
Friary Hill 28 B1
Friary La 28 B1
Frome Ter 28 B1
Garfield Av 28 A3
Gatcombe Clo 29 C3
Gladiator Grn 28 A3
Gloucester Rd 28 A2
Glynde Path Rd 28 B1

Great Western Rd 28 B2
Grey School Pass 28 B1
Grosvenor Cres 28 B3
Grosvenor Rd 28 B3
Hardy Av 29 C1
Hardye Arc 28 B2
Hawthorn Rd 28 A1
Herringston Rd 28 B3
High East St 28 B1
High St 29 C1
High West St 28 B1
Hill Fort Clo 28 A3
Holloway Rd 29 C1
Holly Clo 28 A1
Hutchins Clo 28 A3
Icen Way 28 B1
James Rd 28 A3
Jubilee Ct 28 B1
Kensington Walk 29 C3
Kings Rd 29 C1
Kingsbere Cres 28 B3
Lancaster Rd 28 A3
Legion Clo 28 A3
Lime Clo 28 B2
Linden Av 28 B2
Liscombe Clo 28 A2
Little Britain 29 C2
London Rd 29 C1
Lorne Rd 28 A2
Louis Rd 28 A2
Lubbecke Way 29 C2
Maiden Castle La 28 A3
Malta Clo 28 A1
Manor Rd 28 B3
Margaret Pl 28 A2
Marie Rd 28 A2
Martyr Clo 28 A3
Maud Rd 28 A2
Maumbury Rd 28 B2
Mellstock Av 28 B3
Milford Rd 28 A2
Mill St 29 C1
Millers Clo 28 B1
Minerva Clo 28 B3
Mistover Clo 28 B3
Mithras Clo 28 A3
Monmouth Rd 28 B3
Mountain Ash Rd 28 A1
New Rd 28 A1
New St 28 B2
Normandy Way 28 A1
North Sq 28 B1
Northernhay 28 B1
Olga Rd 28 B2
Orchard St 28 B1
Osborne Clo 29 C2
Piddlehinton Rd 29 C1
Plassey Clo 28 A1
Pound La 29 C2
Poundbury Cres 28 A2
Poundbury Rd 28 A1
Powys Clo 28 A3
Prince of Wales Rd 28 B2
Princes St 28 B2
Prospect Rd 28 A1
Queens Rd 28 A2
Railway Triangle 28 A1
Rampart Walk 28 A3
Remus Clo 28 A3
Riverside Cres 29 C1
Roberts Pl 28 A2
Robins Garth 29 C2
Roman Rd 28 A3
Romulus Clo 28 A3
Rothesay Rd 28 B2
St Georges Clo 29 D2
St Georges Rd 29 C2
St Helens Rd 28 B2
St Thomas Rd 28 A1
Salisbury St 29 C1
Salisbury Walk 29 C2
Sandringham Ct 29 C2
School La 28 B1
Shaston Cres 29 C3
Sherborne Rd 28 B1
Smoky Hole La 29 D2
Somerleigh Rd 28 B2
South Court Av 28 B2
South St 28 B2
South Walks Rd 28 B2
Stinsford Rd 29 D1
Sydenham Way 29 C2
Syward Clo 29 D2
Syward Rd 29 D2
Temple Clo 28 B3
The Grove 28 B1
The Junction 28 A3
Thornhill Clo 28 A3

reves Rd	28 A3
rinity St	28 B1
udor Arc	28 B2
espasian Way	28 A3
icarage La	29 C1
ictoria Rd	28 B2
ictoria Ter	29 C2
Vareham Rd	29 D3
Veatherbury Av	28 B3
Veld Ct	28 B2
Vellbridge Clo	28 B3
Vessex Rd	28 A2
Vessex Way	28 A2
Vest Mills La	28 B1
Vest Stafford Rd	29 D3
Vest Walks	28 B2
Vestover Rd	28 B2
Veymouth Av	28 B3
Veymouth Rd	28 A3
Vhitfield	28 A2
Vilson Rd	29 C2
Vindsor Rd	28 A2
Vollaston Rd	28 B2
Vyvern Rd	28 A1
ork Rd	29 C2

FORTUNESWELL/ EASTON

Albert Ter	30 B1
Alma Ter	30 C2
Amelia Clo	30 B1
Artists Row	30 B2
Augusta Rd	30 C2
Balaclava Rd	30 C1
Parleycroft	31 A3
eel Clo	30 B1
elgrave Pl	30 B1
Bellevue Ter	30 B2
Placknor Rd	31 A3
Blindmere Rd	31 A3
Bloomfield Ter	31 B3
Powers Rd	31 A3
own Hill	30 B1
ranscombe Clo	31 B4
reston Clo	31 B4
Brymers Av	30 B2
umper La	31 C3
astle Rd	30 B1
Castletown	30 B1
edar Dri	31 B4
hannel View Rd	31 B3
harmouth Pl	31 C3
heyne Clo	31 B4
hiswell High St	30 B1
hurch La	31 B4
hurch Ope Rd	31 C3
larence Clo	31 B3
larence Rd	31 B3
lements La	30 B1
lovens Rd	30 B2
oastguard Cotts	30 B1
oastguard Rd	30 B1
oronation Rd	30 B1
ourt Barton Sharpits	31 B3
ourtlands Rd	31 B3
ove Cotts	30 B2
roft Rd	31 A3
elhi La	31 B3
ock Rd	30 B1
ast St	30 B2
ast Wear Rd	30 B1
aston Rd	30 B2
aston Sq	31 B3
ortuneswell	30 B2
our Acres	31 B3
reshwater Clo	31 B4
urlands	31 B3
Grangecroft Rd	31 A3
green Hill Ter	30 B1
reenways	31 B3
rosvenor Rd	31 B3
rove Rd	31 B3
am Croft	31 B3
arbour View Rd	30 B1
aylands	31 B3
eadland Clo	31 B4
igh St	31 B4
ncline Rd	30 C1
nner Breakwater Rd	30 C1
sle Rd	31 B3
illicks Hill	30 B2
ing St	30 B2
angley Clo	31 B4
eet Clo	30 B1
imekiln Clo	31 B4

Long Acre	31 C3
Longstone Clo	31 B4
Main Rd	30 B1
Mallams	30 B1
Martinscroft Rd	31 A3
Mead Bower	31 B4
Merton Ter	30 B2
Montrose Clo	31 B3
Moorfield Rd	31 C3
New Rd	30 B2
New St	31 C3
Old Depot Rd	30 C1
Old Hill	30 B2
Osborne Rd	30 B1
Park Estate Rd	31 B3
Park Rd	31 B3
Pauls Mead	30 B2
Pennsylvania	31 C4
Pound Piece	31 B3
Priory Rd	30 B2
Promenade	30 B1
Providence Pl	31 B4
Queens Rd	30 B1
Railway Rd	31 B3
Reap La	31 A4
Reforne Cl	31 B3
Reforne St	31 B3
Rip Croft	31 A4
Rufus Way	30 C2
Rushetts Clo	31 B4
St Georges Estate Rd	30 B3
St Georges Rd	31 B3
St Martins Rd	30 B2
St Pauls Rd	30 B2
Sea Vw	30 B1
Seven Acres	31 B4
Shepherds Croft	31 C3
Shortlands	31 B3
Southwell St	31 B4
Spring Gdns	30 B2
Straits	31 B3
Sweet Hill La	31 B4
Sweet Hill Rd	31 B4
The Grove	31 C3
Three Yards Clo	30 B2
Tilleycoombe Rd	30 B2
Tobys Clo	31 B3
Underhedge Gdns	31 B4
Ventnor Rd	30 B1
Verne Common Rd	30 B1
Verne Rd	30 B2
Victoria Pl	31 B3
Victoria Rd	30 C2
Victoria Sq	30 A1
Victory Rd	30 B1
Wakeham St	31 C3
Wallsend Clo	31 B4
Weare Clo	30 B2
Westcliff Rd	31 B3
Weston Rd	31 B4
Weston St	31 B4
Westwools	31 B4
Weymouth Rd	30 A1
Wheatlands	31 B4
Wide St	31 A3
Woolcombe Rd	31 A3
Yeats Rd	30 B2
Yeolands Rd	31 B3

GILLINGHAM

Abbotts Way	32 A2
Addison Clo	32 B3
Arun Clo	32 A1
Avondale Gdns	32 A2
Barnaby Mead	32 A2
Bay La	32 B2
Bay Rd	32 A2
Bourne Way	32 A1
Bridge Clo	32 B3
Broad Robin	32 A2
Brookside	32 B1
Buckingham Rd	32 A2
Cemetery Rd	32 A2
Chestnut Way	32 A2
Church Walk	32 A2
Claremont Av	32 A1
Coldharbour	32 A2
Common Mead Av	32 A2
Common Mead La	32 A2
Cordery Gdns	32 A1
Coronation Rd	32 A2
Cypress Way	32 A2
Deweys Way	32 A2
Dolphin La	32 A1
Downsview Dri	32 A1
Fairey Clo	32 A1
Fairey Cres	32 A1

Great House Walk	32 A2
Hardings La	32 A2
Hawthorne Av	32 A2
High St	32 A2
Hyde Rd	32 A2
Juniper Gdns	32 A2
Kings Court Clo	32 B2
Kingscourt Rd	32 B3
Knoll Pl	32 A1
Laburnam Way	32 A3
Lammas Clo	32 A1
Lawrence Cotts	32 B3
Lockwood Ter	32 B3
Lodbourne Grn	32 A2
Lodbourne Ter	32 A2
Maple Way	32 A2
Mathews Pl	32 A2
New Rd	32 B3
Newbury	32 B2
Orchard Rd	32 A2
Peacemarsh	32 A1
Purns Mill La	32 A1
Queen St	32 A2
Railway Ter	32 B2
Rookery Clo	32 B3
St Martins Sq	32 A2
Saxon Mead Clo	32 A1
School La	32 A2
School Rd	32 B2
Shaftesbury Rd	32 B3
Shreen Clo	32 B2
Shreen Way	32 B2
Somerset Clo	32 A1
South St	32 A2
Station Rd	32 B3
Stour Ct	32 A2
Stour Gdns	32 A2
Sycamore Way	32 A2
Sydney Pl	32 A2
Sylvan Clo	32 B1
Sylvan Way	32 A1
The Laurels	32 A2
The Square	32 A2
Tomlins La	32 A2
Turners La	32 A2
Victoria Rd	32 B2
Wavering La	32 A2
Waverland Ter	32 A2
Wessex Way	32 A1
Wiltshire Clo	32 A1
Wyke Rd	32 A2
Wyke St	32 A2

LYME REGIS

Albot Rd	33 B2
Anning Rd	33 B2
Avenue Rd	33 B2
Barbers La	33 A1
Bayview Rd	33 B2
Blue Water Dri	33 A2
Bridge St	33 B3
Broad St	33 B2
Charmouth Clo	33 B2
Charmouth Rd	33 B2
Church St, Lyme Regis	33 B2
Church St, Uplyme	33 A1
Clappentail La	33 A2
Clappentail Pk	33 A2
Cobb Rd	33 B3
Colway La	33 B2
Coombe St	33 B2
Coram Av	33 A3
Corporation Ter	33 B2
Crogg La	33 A1
Dolphins Clo	33 B2
Dragons Hill	33 B1
East Cliff	33 B2
Elizabeth Clo	33 B2
Fairfield Pk	33 B2
Ferndown Rd	33 B2
Georges Ct	33 B3
Gore La	33 A2
Greenway	33 A2
Haye Clo	33 A2
Haye La	33 A1
High Cliff Rd	33 A2
Hill Rise Rd	33 B2
Hill Road	33 B2
Kings Way	33 B2
Limekiln La	33 A1
Long Entry	33 B2
Lym Clo	33 B2
Lynch Mill La	33 B2
Manor Av	33 B2
Marine Par	33 B2
Mill Green	33 B2
Mill La	33 A2

Monmouth St	33 B2
North Av	33 B2
Ozone Ter	33 B3
Penny Plot	33 A2
Pine Ridge	33 B2
Pine Walk	33 A3
Pooles Ct	33 B2
Portland Ct	33 A2
Pound La	33 A1
Pound Rd	33 B2
Pound St	33 B2
Prospect Pl	33 B2
Queens Walk	33 B2
Roman Rd	33 B2
Sherborne La	33 B2
Shire La	33 A2
Sidmouth Rd	33 A2
Silver St	33 B2
Somer Fields	33 A2
Somers Rd	33 A2
South Av	33 B2
Spittles La	33 B2
Springhead Rd	33 A1
Springhill Gdns	33 B2
Staples Ter	33 B2
Stile La	33 B3
Summerhill Rd	33 B2
Tappers Knap	33 A1
Timber Hill	33 B2
Uplyme Rd	33 A1
Upper Westhill Rd	33 A2
Venlake La	33 A1
View Rd	33 B2
Ware La	33 A3
Westhill Rd	33 A2
Whalley La	33 A1
Windsor Ter	33 B2
Woodmead Rd	33 B2

LYTCHETT MATRAVERS

Ancott Clo	34 B1
Blandford Rd Nth	34 C1
Castle Farm Rd	34 A1
Deans Drove	34 B2
Dillons Gdns	34 A2
Eddygreen Rd	34 A2
Eldons Drove	34 A1
Flowers Drove	34 B1
Foxhills Cres	34 B1
Foxhills La	34 B2
Frys Clo	34 B1
Glebe Rd	34 A2
Hannams Clo	34 B1
High St	34 A1
Hopmans Clo	34 A1
Huntick Rd	34 B1
Hunticks Estate	34 B1
Lime Kiln Rd	34 B1
Lockyers Way	34 B2
Middle Rd	34 A2
Old Chapel Dri	34 B1
Old Pound Clo	34 A1
Poole Rd	34 C1
Prospect Rd	34 B2
Purbeck Rd	34 B1
Scutts Clo	34 B1
The Spinney	34 B2
Vineyard Clo	34 B1
Wareham Rd	34 A2
Wimborne Rd	34 B1

LYTCHETT MINSTER

Dorchester Rd	35 A2
Huntick Rd	35 B1
Lychett Minster By-Pass	35 A2
New Rd	35 A1
Policemans La	35 B1
Post Green La	35 A2
Slough La	35 B2
Watery la	35 B2

MAIDEN NEWTON

Ashley Av	35 B3
Back La	35 A4
Bull La	35 B4
Cattistock Rd	35 B3
Chapel La	35 B3
Chilfrome La	35 A3
Church Rd	35 B3

Cruxton La	35 B4		
Dorchester Rd	35 A3		
Drift Rd	35 B3		
Frome La	35 B4		
Frome Vw	35 B4		
Glebe Clo	35 B4		
Greenford La	35 A4		
Greenford Vw	35 A3		
Harvey Clo	35 B4		
Hill Vw	35 B4		
Newton Rd	35 B4		
Norden La	35 B3		
North Rd	35 B3		
Pound Piece	35 B3		
Stanstead Rd	35 B4		
Station Rd	35 B3		
Webbers Piece	35 B3		

POOLE

Adelaide Rd	36 B2		
Ballard Clo	36 B3		
Ballard Rd	36 B3		
Bay Hog La	36 A3		
Bennetts Alley	36 A3		
Blandford Rd	36 A3		
Bracken Glen	36 B2		
Brailswood Rd	36 B2		
Brampton Rd	36 B1		
Briar Clo	36 B1		
Bridge Approach	36 A3		
Bright Rd	36 B2		
Broadstone Way	36 A1		
Canford Rd	36 B2		
Carters La	36 A3		
Castle St	36 A3		
Catalina Dri	36 B3		
Chapel La	36 B3		
Charles Rd	36 B2		
Christopher Cres	36 A1		
Church St	36 A3		
Churchfield Rd	36 B2		
Cinnamon La	36 A3		
Cobbs La	36 B1		
Colbourne Clo	36 B3		
Connell Rd	36 B1		
Cranes Mews	36 B2		
Curlieu Rd	36 B1		
Darbys Clo	36 B1		
Darbys La	36 B1		
Dear Hay La	36 A3		
Dee Way	36 A3		
Denby Rd	36 B2		
Denmark La	36 B2		
Denmark Rd	36 B2		
Dingley Rd	36 B1		
Dorchester Rd	36 B1		
Drake Rd	36 B3		
East Quay Rd	36 B3		
East St	36 B3		
Elizabeth Rd	36 B2		
Emerson Clo	36 B3		
Emerson Rd	36 B3		
Enfield Rd	36 B1		
Esplanade	36 B2		
Falkland Sq	36 B3		
Fernside Rd	36 B1		
Ferry Rd	36 A3		
Fishermans Rd	36 B3		
Fleets Lane	36 A1		
Furnell Rd	36 B3		
Garland Rd	36 B2		
Globe La	36 B3		
Green Clo	36 B3		
Green Rd	36 B3		
Harbour Hill Cres	36 B1		
Haynes Av	36 B2		
Heath Av	36 B1		
Heckford Rd	36 B2		
Hennings Park Rd	36 B1		
High St	36 A3		
Hiley Rd	36 B1		
Hill St	36 A3		
Holes Bay Rd	36 A1		
Ivor Rd	36 A3		
Jolliffe Av	36 B2		
Jolliffe Rd	36 B2		
Kingland Cres	36 B3		
Kingland Rd	36 B2		
Kings Bere Rd	36 B1		
Kingston Rd	36 B2		
Labrador Dri	36 B3		
Lander Clo	36 B3		
Langland St	36 B3		
Levets La	36 A3		
Maple Rd	36 B2		
Market Clo	36 A3		
Market St	36 A3		

Marlott Rd	36 B1		
Marnhull Rd	36 B2		
Marston Rd	36 A3		
Mellstock Rd	36 B1		
Middle Rd	36 B1		
Milestone Rd	36 B1		
Mount Pleasant Av	36 B2		
Nansen Av	36 B1		
New Harbour Rd	36 A3		
New Orchard	36 A3		
New Quay Rd	36 A3		
New St	36 A3		
Newfoundland Dri	36 B3		
North St	36 B3		
Oakdale Rd	36 B1		
Oakfield Rd	36 B1		
Old Orchard	36 A3		
Palmer Rd	36 A1		
Paradise St	36 A3		
Parish Rd	36 B2		
Park Lake Rd	36 B3		
Parkstone Rd	36 B2		
Perry Gdns	36 B3		
Pitwines Clo	36 B3		
Popes Rd	36 B1		
Pound La	36 A3		
Preston Rd	36 B1		
Prosperous St	36 B3		
Rectory Rd	36 A1		
Rigler Rd	36 A3		
Rowland Av	36 B1		
St Aubyns Ct	36 A3		
St James Clo	36 A3		
St Johns Rd	36 B2		
St Margarets Rd	36 B2		
St Marys Rd	36 B2		
Sandbourne	36 B2		
Sandpits La	36 B2		
Sarum St	36 A3		
Seldown La	36 B2		
Seldown Rd	36 B2		
Seliot Clo	36 B1		
Serpentine La N	36 B2		
Serpentine La S	36 B2		
Serpentine Rd	36 B2		
Shaftesbury Rd	36 B2		
Shapwick Rd	36 A3		
Sherrin Clo	36 B1		
Shottsford Rd	36 B1		
Simmonds Clo	36 B1		
Skinner St	36 B3		
Slip Way	36 A3		
Somerby Rd	36 B1		
Stanley Green Rd	36 A1		
Stanley Rd	36 B3		
Staple Close La	36 B1		
Station Rd	36 A3		
Stenhurst Rd	36 B1		
Sterte Av	36 A2		
Sterte Clo	36 B2		
Sterte Rd	36 B2		
Stokes Av	36 B2		
Strand St	36 A3		
Tatnam La	36 B2		
Tatnam Rd	36 B2		
Tavener Clo	36 B3		
Thames St	36 A3		
The Quay	36 A3		
Towngate Bridge	36 B3		
Vallis Clo	36 B3		
Vicarage Rd	36 B1		
Waldron Clo	36 B3		
Well La	36 B1		
West Quay Rd	36 A3		
West St	36 A3		
West View Rd	36 B2		
Westons La	36 B3		
Whatleigh Clo	36 B3		
White Horse Dri	36 B1		
Whittles Way	36 A3		
Wilkins Way	36 A3		
Willis Way	36 A1		
Wimborne Rd	36 B1		
Wingfield Av	36 B1		
Winifred Rd	36 B1		
Winterbourne Clo	36 B1		
Winterbourne Rd	36 B1		

PRESTON

Barton Dri	37 A2		
Baydon Clo	37 A2		
Bridge Inn Rd	37 B2		
Brookside Clo	37 A2		
Brunel Dri	37 A2		
Cedar Dri	37 A2		

Chalbury Clo	37 A2		
Church Rd	37 B2		
Churchward Av	37 A2		
Collet Clo	37 A2		
Coombe Valley Rd	37 A1		
Fir Dri	37 A2		
Fisherbridge Rd	37 B2		
Hambro Ter	37 B2		
Hawksworth Clo	37 A2		
Holcombe Clo	37 B2		
Horyford Clo	37 B2		
Littlemoor Rd	37 A2		
Maunsell Av	37 A2		
Medway Dri	37 A2		
Millers Clo	37 A1		
Mission Hall La	37 B1		
Moorcombe Dri	37 A2		
Old Bincombe La	37 B1		
Old Granary Clo	37 A1		
Plaisters La	37 B1		
Preston Rd	37 A2		
Puddledock La	37 A2		
Reynards Way	37 A1		
Rhosewood Dri	37 A2		
Seven Acres	37 A2		
Silver St	37 B1		
Stanier Rd	37 A2		
Stroudley Cres	37 A2		
Sutton Clo	37 B1		
Sutton Court Lawns	37 B1		
Sutton Pk	37 B2		
Sutton Rd	37 B1		
Telford Clo	37 A2		
Verlands Rd	37 B2		
Wainwright Clo	37 A2		
White Horse Dri	37 B2		
Willow Cres	37 A2		
Winslow Rd	37 B1		

PUDDLETOWN

Athelhampton Rd	37 B4		
Beech Rd	37 B4		
Bellbury Clo	37 B4		
Brymer Rd	37 A4		
Butt Clo	37 B4		
Charminster La	37 A3		
Chine Hill La	37 A3		
Cobbs Pl	37 B4		
Coombe Rd	37 A4		
Druce La	37 A3		
High St	37 A3		
Mill St	37 B4		
Millom La	37 B4		
New St	37 A4		
Rod Hill La	37 A4		
Styles La	37 A3		
The Green	37 B4		
The Moor	37 A3		
The Square	37 B3		
Thompson Clo	37 A3		
Walpole Ct	37 B3		
White Hill	37 A4		
Willoughby Clo	37 A4		

SHAFTESBURY

Abbey Clo	38 B2		
Abbey Walk	38 B2		
Angel La	38 B1		
Ash Clo	38 B1		
Barton Clo	38 B1		
Barton Hill	38 B1		
Bell St	38 B1		
Belmont Clo	38 B2		
Bimport	38 A2		
Blackmore Rd	38 C1		
Bleke St	38 B1		
Boundary Rd	38 B2		
Boyne Mead	38 B2		
Boyne Mead Clo	38 B2		
Breach La	38 A2		
Brinscombe La	38 B2		
Butts Mead	38 B2		
Calves La	38 A1		
Castle Hill Clo	38 A1		
Christys La	38 B1		
Church Hill	38 A1		
Church Walk	38 B2		
Coppice St	38 B1		
Cranbourne Dri	38 B1		
Crookhays	38 B1		
Dark La	38 B1		
Fairlane	38 C2		
Fountains Mead	38 B1		
Foyle Hill	38 A2		
French Mill Rise	38 B2		
Frenchmill La	38 B2		

Gillingham Rd	38	
Gold Hill	38	
Granville Gdns	38	
Great La	38	
Grosvenor Rd	38	
Haimes La	38	
Hawkesdene	38	
Hawkesdene La	38	
Hawthorne Clo	38	
Heathfields Way	38	
High St	38	
Higher Blandford Rd	38	
Homefield	38	
Horse Ponds	38	
Jubilee Walk	38	
Kingsman La	38	
Laneside	38	
Langfords La	38	
Laundry La	38	
Layton La	38	
Linden Park	38	
Lindlar Clo	38	
Little Content La	38	
Little Down	38	
Long Cross	38	
Long Mead	38	
Love La	38	
Lower Blandford Rd	38	
Lyons Walk	38	
Magdalane La	38	
Mampitts La	38	
Mampitts Rd	38	
Maple Clo	38	
Meadow Clo	38	
Motcombe Rd	38	
Mustons La	38	
Nettlebed Nursery	38	
Nettlecombe	38	
New La	38	
New Rd	38	
Old St	38	
Oxencroft	38	
Paddock Clo	38	
Park La	38	
Park Walk	38	
Parsons Pool	38	
Pine Walk	38	
Pix Mead	38	
Raspberry La	38	
Ratcliffs Gdns	38	
Ridgeway	38	
Rowan Clo	38	
Rumbolds Rd	38	
St Edwards Clo	38	
St Georges Rd	38	
St James St	38	
St Jameses Common	38	
St Johns Hill	38	
St Lawrences Cres	38	
St Martins La	38	
Salisbury Rd	38	
Salisbury St	38	
Sally Kings La	38	
Saxon Spur	38	
Shaftesbury By-Pass	38	
Shiphouse La	38	
Shooters La	38	
Snakey La	38	
Spring Field	38	
Stokey Path	38	
Sturminster	38	
Sweetmans Rd	38	
Tanyard La	38	
Ten Acres	38	
The Beeches	38	
The Butts	38	
The Commons	38	
The Knapp	38	
The Sycamores	38	
The Venn	38	
Tout Hill	38	
Umbers Hill	38	
Victoria St	38	
Watery La	38	
Well La	38	
Westminster Clo	38	
Whitehart La	38	
Wincombe La	38	
Windmill Clo	38	
Woolands	38	
Yeatmans Clo	38	
Yeatmans La	38	

SHERBORNE

Abbey Clo	39	
Abbey Rd	39	
Abbots Way	39	

eman Ct	39 B1
eman Pl	39 B2
eman St	39 B1
kwith Clo	39 A2
ck La	39 B1
rton Gdns	39 A1
ackberry La	39 B1
adford Rd	39 A2
dewell Ct	39 B2
stol Rd	39 B1
stle Rd	39 C1
stle Town Way	39 C1
stleton	39 C1
stleton Rd	39 C1
andlers	39 C1
eap St	39 B1
rysanthemum Row	39 C1
urch La	39 B2
nfield	39 A2
dharbour	39 B1
oks La	39 B2
ombe Rd	39 A1
rnhill	39 B1
lvers Clo	39 B2
aby Rd	39 B2
rchester Rd	39 B2
rrant Pl	39 B2
ls Clo	39 C1
st Mill La	39 C2
ge La	39 B2
sters	39 C1
s House La	39 C2
orge St	39 B1
avel Pits	39 B2
eenhill	39 B1
lf Acres	39 B2
f Moon La	39 B2
f Moon St	39 B2
rbour Rd	39 C1
rbour Way	39 B1
rdings House La	39 A1
her Cheap St	39 B1
hmore Rd	39 A1
Brow	39 A2
House Clo	39 C1
neycombe Rise	39 A2
rsecastles	39 B2
rsecastles La	39 A1
spital La	39 B1
und St	39 B2
nts Mead	39 A2
gs Cres	39 B1
gs Rd	39 B1
Hill	39 B1
ngdons	39 C1
t Ct	39 A2
nthay Clo	39 A2
nthay Rd	39 A2
lefield	39 A2
ng St	39 B2
ver Acreman St	39 B2
tbourne Rd	39 C2
rston Rd	39 A1
Creery Rd	39 B1
hercombe La	39 A1
w Rd	39 B2
well	39 B1
wland	39 B1
wland Dri	39 C1
th Rd	39 B1
orne Rd	39 C2
Farm East & West	39 B1
ery La	39 B2
geant Dri	39 B2
ford La	39 C1
vys La	39 B2
estlands	39 B1
estlands La	39 B1
arr La	39 B1
arr Rd	39 B1
eigh Ct	39 C2
hmond Clo	39 B2
hmond Grn	39 B2
hmond Rd	39 B2
geway	39 A2
Catherines Cres	39 A2
Marys Rd	39 A2
Pauls Clo	39 C1
Pauls Grn	39 B1
Swithins Clo	39 C1
Swithins Rd	39 C1
hool La	39 B2
eeplands La	39 A1
hons Rd	39 B1
uth Av	39 A2
uth Ct	39 A2
uth St	39 B2

Springfield Cres	39 B2
Station Rd	39 B2
Stonedene	39 B1
Swan Yard	39 B1
The Avenue	39 C1
The Green	39 B1
The Hayes	39 B2
The Maltings	39 C2
The Sheeplands	39 A1
The Wilderness	39 C1
Tinneys La	39 C1
Trendle St	39 B2
Trent Path La	39 A1
Vernalls Rd	39 B1
West Mill La	39 B2
Westbridge Pk	39 A2
Westbury	39 B2
Westfield	39 A2
Widforth Clo	39 A2
Wingfield Rd	39 B2
Wootton Gro	39 B1
Wynnes Clo	39 A2
Wynnes Rise	39 A2
Yeovil Rd	39 A2

SHILLINGSTONE CHILD OKEFORD

Apple Acre	40 B1
Blandford Rd	40 A3
Brodham Way	40 A3
Chalwell	40 B2
Church Rd	40 A3
Cookswell	40 A2
Coombe Rd	40 A3
Duck St	40 B2
Everetts La	40 A3
Gold Hill	40 A1
Greenway	40 B1
Greenway La	40 A3
Gunn La	40 A3
Hayward La	40 B1
High St	40 B1
Hine Town La	40 A3
Holloway	40 B3
Homefield	40 A3
Honeysuckle Gdns	40 A3
Jacobs Ladder	40 B1
Knapps	40 A2
Knotts Clo	40 B1
Lanchards	40 A3
Lanchards La	40 A3
Little La	40 A2
Melway Gdns	40 B2
Melway La	40 B2
Millbrook Clo	40 B1
Netmead La	40 A1
Nutmead Clo	40 B1
Olivers Mead	40 B1
Pepper Hill	40 A3
Poplar Hill	40 A3
Portman Dri	40 B1
Puxey La	40 A3
Rectory La	40 B1
Ridgeway La	40 B1
Sandy La	40 B1
Shaftesbury Rd	40 B1
Shillingstone La	40 A3
Southfield La	40 A2
Station Rd	40 B2
Stour Clo	40 B3
The Cross, Child Okeford	40 B1
The Cross, Shillingstone	40 A3
The Hollow	40 B1
Upper Street	40 B1
Wessex Av	40 A3

STALBRIDGE

Barrow Hill	41 A2
Blackmore Rd	41 B1
Boyle Clo	41 B1
Cale Clo	41 B2
Church Hill	41 A1
Church Walk	41 A1
Coppern Way	41 B2
Drews La	41 A1
Duck La	41 A1
Duncliffe Clo	41 A1
Gold St	41 A1
Grosvenor Rd	41 A2
Grove La	41 A1
Grove La Clo	41 A2
Hardy Cres	41 B1
High St	41 A1

Jarvis Clo	41 B2
Jarvis Way	41 B1
Lower Rd	41 B2
Meadow Clo	41 B2
New Rd	41 B2
Park Gro	41 A2
Park Rd	41 A2
Pound Clo	41 A2
Raleigh Rd	41 B2
Ring St	41 B2
Robinson Heights	41 B2
Silk House Barton	41 A1
Stalbridge Clo	41 A2
Station Rd	41 A1
Sturminster Rd	41 B2
Vale Rd	41 B2
Waterlake	41 B2
Wessex Rd	41 B2
Wood La	41 A2

STURMINSTER NEWTON

Alder Clo	41 B3
Alder Rd	41 B3
Barnes Clo	41 A3
Bath Rd	41 A3
Bridge St	41 A4
Brinsley Clo	41 A3
Brinsley Ct	41 A3
Brinsley Mead	41 A3
Butts Pond	41 A3
Church La	41 A4
Church St	41 A4
Church Walk	41 A4
Denhall Clo	41 A3
Durrant	41 A4
Filbridge Rise	41 B3
Friars Moor	41 B4
Gotts La	41 A4
Goughs Clo	41 A3
Green Clo	41 B3
Hambledon View	41 B3
Hanover Clo	41 A3
Honey Mead La	41 B3
Lower Rixon	41 B3
Manston Rd	41 B3
Market Pl	41 A4
Penny St	41 A4
Pitts Orchard	41 A3
Ricketts La	41 A4
Rixon Hill	41 B3
Shortedge	41 B3
Station Rd	41 A3
The Row	41 A3
The Square	41 A4
West End	41 A3
White Lane Clo	41 A3

SWANAGE/ LANGTON MATRAVERS

Aigburth Rd	43 C2
Alderbury Clo	42 B2
Ancaster Rd	43 C2
Anglebury Av	43 C1
Anvil Clo	42 B2
Argyle Rd	43 C2
Atlantic Rd	43 C3
Ballard Est	43 D1
Ballard Lee	43 D1
Ballard Rd	43 D1
Ballard Way	43 D1
Battlegate Rd	43 D2
Battlemead	43 C1
Bay Clo	43 D1
Bay Cres	43 D1
Beach Gdns	43 C2
Bell St	42 B2
Belle Vue Rd	43 D3
Belvedere Rd	43 D3
Benlease Way	42 B2
Bon Accord Rd	43 C3
Bonfields Av	43 C1
Brickyard La	43 C1
Broad Rd	43 D2
Burlington Rd	43 D1
Cauldon Av	43 C2
Cauldon Barn Rd	43 C1
Cauldon Cres	43 C1
Cecil Rd	43 C2
Chapel La	43 C2
Church Hill	43 C2
Cliff Av	43 D1
Cluny Cres	43 D2

Combe Hill	42 A2
Commercial Rd	43 D2
Cornwall Rd	43 C2
Court Hill	43 C2
Court Rd	43 C2
Cowlease	43 C2
Crack La	42 A2
Cranborne Rd	43 C2
Cufton Rd	43 D1
D'Urberville Dri	43 C1
Darkie La	43 C1
Days Rd	42 B2
De Moulham Rd	43 D1
Drummond Rd	43 D3
Durlston Rd	43 D3
Durnford Drove	42 A3
Durnford Pl	43 C2
Eldon Ter	43 C2
Exeter Rd	43 D2
Findlay Pl	43 C2
Gannetts Pk	43 C2
Gilbert Rd	43 C2
Globe Clo	43 C2
Godlingston La	42 B1
Gordon Rd	43 D2
Grosvenor Rd	43 D3
Gypshayes	42 A2
Hendrie Clo	43 C2
High Cliff Rd	43 D1
High St, Langton Matravers	42 A2
High St, Swanage	42 B2
Hill Rd	43 C1
Hillsea Rd	43 C2
Hillview Rd	43 C2
Hoborne Rd	43 C2
Holmes Rd	42 B2
Howard Rd	43 C2
Ilminster Rd	43 C2
Institute Rd	43 D2
Jubilee Rd	42 B2
Kings Rd East	43 D2
Kings Rd West	43 D2
Kingswood Clo	42 B2
Knolsea Clo	43 D3
Leeson Clo	42 B2
Lighthouse Rd	43 D3
Linden Rd	43 C2
Locarno Rd	43 C2
Manor Rd	43 D2
Manwell Dri	43 C3
Manwell Rd	43 C2
Mariners Dri	43 C2
Marshall Row	43 D2
Mermaid Rd	43 D2
Moor Rd	43 C1
Morriston Rd	43 C2
Mount Pleasant La	43 D2
Mount Scars	43 C3
Newbury Rd	43 C2
Newton Clo	43 C2
Newton Rd	43 D2
Northbrook Rd	43 C1
Osborne Rd	43 C2
Osmay Rd	43 D3
Panorama Rd	43 C2
Park Rd	43 D2
Peveril Rd	43 D3
Priests Rd	43 C2
Priests Way	42 B3
Princess Rd	43 C2
Prospect Cres	43 C2
Purbeck Ter Rd	43 D3
Purbeck Vw	43 C2
Quarry Clo	43 C2
Queens Mead	43 C2
Queens Rd	43 C2
Rabling Rd	43 C2
Redcliff Rd	43 D1
Rempstone Back Rd	43 C2
Rempstone Rd	43 D2
Richmond Rd	43 C3
Rough Height	43 C3
Russell Av	43 D3
St Vast Rd	43 D3
Salisbury Rd	43 D3
Sentry Rd	43 D2
Seymer Rd	43 C2
Shirley Clo	43 C2
Shore Rd	43 D2
Solent Rd	43 D3
South Cliff Rd	43 D3
South Rd	43 C2
Springfield Rd	43 C2
Stafford Rd	43 D2
Station Pl	43 D2
Station Rd	43 D2
Steer Rd	43 C2

Streche Rd 43 D1
Sundridge Clo 43 C3
Sunnydale Rd 43 D3
Sunshine Walk 43 C2
Sydenham Rd 43 B2
Taunton Rd 43 D2
The Hyde 43 A2
The Parade 43 D2
Three Acre La 42 A2
Toms Field 42 A2
Townsend Rd 43 C2
Ulwell Rd 43 C1
Valley Rd 42 A2
Victoria Av 42 B2
Victoria Rd 43 D1
Vivian Pk 43 C1
Walrond Rd 43 C2
Washpond La, Langton
  Matravers 42 B1
Washpond La,
  New Swanage 43 C1
Wessex Way 43 C1
West Dri 43 C2
Whitecliff Rd 43 C1
Wills Rd 43 C2
York Ter 43 D2

UPWEY BROADWEY

Beech Rd 47 A3
Beverley Rd 47 B3
Brambling Clo 47 B3
Bridlebank Way 47 B3
Broadway Clo 47 B3
Camedown Clo 47 B3
Chaffinch Clo 47 B3
Chapel La 47 B2
Church St 47 A1
Clatton Clo 47 B3
Dorchester Rd 47 A3
Elwell St 47 A2
Fieldfare Clo 47 B3
Firecrest Clo 47 B3
Friar Waddon La 47 A1
Georgian Clo 47 B3
Goldcrest Clo 47 B3
Goulds Hill 47 A1
Icen La 47 B3
Jenner Way 47 B3
Jestys Av 47 B3
Jordan Way 47 B3
Juniper Way 47 B3
Kestrel Vw 47 B3
Kinley Rd 47 B3
Little Mead 47 A3
Littlemoor Rd 47 A3
Lorton La 47 A3
Louviers Rd 47 B3
Meadow View Rd 47 B3
Meredin Clo 47 B3
Mill St 47 A3
Nightingale Dri 47 B3
North Merlin Av 47 A3
Nuthatch Clo 47 B3
Old Roman Rd 47 B1
Old Station Rd 47 B3
Pemberton Clo 47 B3
Pipit Clo 47 B3
Prospect Pl 47 B2
Redpoll Clo 47 B3
Reedlings Clo 47 B3
Regency Dri 47 B3
Ridgeway 47 B2
Ridgeway Hill 47 B2
Robin Clo 47 B3
Rockhampton Clo 47 B3
St Helier Av 47 B3
St Julien Cres 47 A3
St Lawrence Rd 47 B2
Sanderling Clo 47 B3
Selwyn Clo 47 B3
Shortlands Rd 47 B2
South Merlin Av 47 A3
Springfield Clo 47 B3
Springfield Rd 47 A3
Stonechat Clo 47 B3
Stottingway St 47 A2
The Doves 47 B3
The Finches 47 B3
The Orchard 47 A3
The Woodpeckers 47 B3
Thurnstone Clo 47 B3
Victoria Av 47 B2
Watery La 47 A3
Westlake Rd 47 B3
Weyview Cres 47 A3

Wheatear Clo 47 B3
Windsor Rd 47 B3

VERWOOD

Aggis Farm Rd 44 B1
Aspen Dri 44 C1
Badger Way 44 B2
Bakers Farm Rd 44 B1
Beech Clo 44 B2
Belmont Clo 44 B2
Berkeley Clo 44 A1
Bingham Clo 44 C2
Bingham Dri 44 C2
Bingham Rd 44 C2
Bitterne Way 44 C2
Black Hill 44 C1
Blackthorn Way 44 C2
Bridport Rd 44 B2
Brook Dri 44 C2
Bugdens La 44 B1
Burley Clo 44 C2
Burn Clo 44 C2
Burnbake Rd 44 B2
Burrows La 44 B1
Carne Dri 44 B1
Cartref Clo 44 B1
Chestnut Clo 44 C2
Chiltern Dri 44 B2
Church Hill 44 B1
Churchfields 44 B1
Claylake Dri 44 C2
Coniston Clo 44 B1
Coronation Rd 44 B1
Cotswold Clo 44 B2
Crescent Rd 44 C1
Dewlands Rd 44 A2
Dewlands Way 44 A1
Eastworth Rd 44 B1
Edmondsham Rd 44 B1
Firs Glen Rd 44 B2
Forge La 44 A2
Foxes Clo 44 B2
Foxhills 44 C1
Glenwood Rd 44 B2
Hayward Cres 44 B2
Hayward Farm Clo 44 B2
Hayward Way 44 A2
Hazelwood Dri 44 C2
Hillside Rd 44 B1
Holly Gro 44 A2
Home Farm Rd 44 B1
Home Farm Way 44 B1
Honeyfly Rd 44 C2
Horton Way 44 A2
Howard Rd 44 B1
Howe La 44 B2
Jessica Av 44 A1
Keswick Way 44 B2
Lake Rd 44 C2
Lancaster Dri 44 B2
Lombardy Clo 44 C2
Manor Rd 44 B1
Manor Way 44 B1
Margards La 44 A2
Meadow Gro 44 C2
Meadow Way 44 C2
Mendip Rd 44 B1
Monmouth Clo 44 C2
Monmouth Dri 44 C2
Moorlands Rd 44 B1
Newtons Rd 44 C1
Newtown La 44 B2
Nightingale Clo 44 C2
Noon Gdns 44 C1
Noon Hill Dri 44 C1
Noon Hill Rd 44 C1
Oaklands Clo 44 B1
Otter Clo 44 C2
Owls Rd 44 C2
Park Dri 44 B1
Pennine Way 44 B2
Penrith Clo 44 B2
Pine View Clo 44 A1
Pine View Rd 44 A1
Potterne Way 44 C2
Purbeck Dri 44 B2
Raymond Clo 44 C1
Redmans Vw 44 A1
Ringwood Rd 44 B1
Rowan Dri 44 C2
St Michaels Clo 44 B2
St Michaels Rd 44 B2
St Stephens La 44 C1
Sandy La 44 C1
Shard Clo 44 C1
Sherwood Dri 44 C1
Sleepbrook Clo 44 B1

Southernhay Rd 44 C1
Springfield Clo 44 B2
Springfield Rd 44 B2
Squirrel Walk 44 B2
Stanley Clo 44 C2
Station Rd 44 A1
Strathmore Dri 44 C1
The Chase 44 C1
The Curlews 44 C2
The Grove 44 C2
The Kingfishers 44 C2
The Lea 44 C2
The Oaks 44 B1
Verne Rd 44 C2
Vicarage Rd 44 B1
West Clo 44 A1
Whitebeam Way 44 C2
Woodlinken Clo 44 C2
Woodlinken Dri 44 C2
Woodlinken Way 44 C2
Woodpecker Clo 44 B2

WAREHAM

Abbots Quay 45 A3
Admirals Way 45 B2
Avon Dri 45 A2
Barnes Rd 45 A3
Bells Orchard 45 B3
Bells Orchard La 45 B3
Bere Rd 45 A2
Bestwall Cres 45 B3
Bestwell Rd 45 B3
Bonnets La 45 A3
Bourne Dri 45 A2
Brixeys La 45 A3
Bryn Rd 45 B1
Burns Rd 45 A2
Carey Clo 45 A2
Carey Rd 45 A2
Carrion La 45 A3
Church Ct 45 B3
Church Grn 45 A3
Church La 45 B3
Church St 45 B3
Connigar La 45 B3
Courtenay Clo 45 B2
Cow La 45 A3
Dollins La 45 A3
Drax Av 45 A2
East St 45 A3
East Walls 45 B3
Edward Cres 45 B3
Egdon Rd 45 A2
Elmwood Clo 45 B1
Encombe Rd 45 A3
Fairway Dri 45 A2
Filleul Rd 45 B1
Frome Rd 45 A3
Gore Hill 45 B1
Great Loven Dri 45 A1
Hardy Rd 45 A3
Howards La 45 A3
Johns Rd 45 A2
Keysworth Dri 45 B1
Mellstock Cres 45 A2
Middle Bere Dri 45 A2
Miles Av 45 B1
Mill La 45 A3
Mistover Rd 45 A2
Monmouth Rd 45 A3
Morden Rd 45 B1
Moretons La 45 A3
New St 45 A3
Norden Dri 45 A2
North Causeway 45 A2
North St 45 A3
North Walls 45 A3
Northmoor Way 45 A2
Northport Dri 45 A2
Peak Vale 45 A2
Pleasant Folly La 45 A3
Pound La 45 A3
Rodgett Cres 45 B1
Ropers La 45 A3
Ryan Clo 45 A2
St Helens Rd 45 B1
St Johns Hill 45 A3
St Martins La 45 A3
St Martins Rd 45 B1
St Marys Clo 45 A2
St Michaels Rd 45 A3
Sandford La 45 A2
Sandford Rd 45 A2
Seven Barrows Rd 45 A3
Shatters Hill 45 A3
Sherford Dri 45 A2
Shirley Rd 45 A3

South Causeway 45 A
South St 45 A
Stockley Rd 45 A
Stour Dri 45 A
Stowell Cres 45 A
Streche Rd 45 A
Tamlin St 45 A
Tanners La 45 A
Tantinoby La 45 A
Tarrant Rd 45 A
The Quay 45 A
Tinkers La 45 A
Trent Dri 45 A
Trinity La 45 A
Tyneham Clo 45 A
Walls View Rd 45 A
Wareham By-Pass 45 A
Wellstead Rd 45 A
Wessex Oval 45 A
West Mill Cres 45 A
West St 45 A
West Walls 45 A
Westminster Rd 45 A
Westport Rd 45 A
Worgret Rd 45 A
Wyatts La 45 A

WEST LULWORTH

Bindon Clo 46 A
Bindon Rd 46 A
Church Hill 46 A
Farm Rd 46 A
School La 46 A
Shepherds Way 46 A
Sunnyside Rd 46 A
The Launches 46 A
Vale Rd 46 A

WEST MOORS

Abbey Rd 52
Arnold Clo 52
Arnold Rd 52
Ashurst Rd 52
Avon Rd 52
Beaufoys Av 52
Beechwood Rd 52
Belle Vue Gro 52
Birch Gro 52
Bond Av 52
Braeside Rd 52
Canterbury Clo 52
Charnwood Clo 52
Compton Cres 52
Cranleigh Pk 52
Denewood Copse 52
Denewood Rd 52
Edgemoor Rd 52
Elmhurst Rd 52
Elmhurst Way 52
Farm Rd 52
Ferndown By-Pass 52
Fernside Rd 52
Fir Clo 52
Firs Glen Rd 52
Forest Rd 52
Glenwood Clo 52
Glenwood La 52
Glenwood Rd 52
Glenwood Way 52
Hardy Clo 52
Hardy Rd 52
Heatherdown Rd 52
Heatherdown Way 52
Heathfield Rd 52
Heathfield Way 52
Heston Way 52
Highfield Rd 52
Kingfisher Clo 52
Kings Clo 52
Maloren Way 52
Martins Dri 52
Merino Way 52
Milford Clo 52
Monks Clo 52
Moorlands Rise 52
Moorlands Road 52
Moorside Rd 52
Newmans La 52
Oakhurst Clo 52
Oakhurst La 52
Oakhurst Rd 52
Pennington Clo 52
Pennington Cres 52
Pennington Rd 52
Pinehurst Rd 52

'y Rd 52 B3
ens Clo 52 A3
ie Pl 52 A1
wood Rd 52 B3
rside Rd 52 A2
m Av 52 A1
'tesbury Clo 52 A2
'tesbury Rd 52 A2
ey Clo 52 A2
hdown Way 52 A3
hern Av 52 B3
ners Clo 52 A3
on Rd 52 A1
mercroft Way 52 A2
el Way 52 A3
Avenue 52 A2
nds Clo 52 B3
nds Rd 52 B2
vers Clo 52 A3
t Moors 52 A3
t Moors Rd 52 A1
dside Rd 52 A1
lslope Clo 52 A3
lslope Gdns 52 A3
lslope Rd 52 A3

EYMOUTH

otsbury Rd 50 B1
cia Clo 48 A3
aide Cres 50 B1
ny Rd 50 A1
ert St,
oucester Mews 51 C1
andra Gdns 51 C2
andra Rd, Radipole 48 B3
andra Rd,
eymouth Sth 50 A1
Saints Rd 50 A2
a Rd 51 C1
ond Gro 48 A3
oleside 48 A2
etree Clo 48 B2
gon Clo 50 B3
yle Rd 48 B3
ngton 48 A3
Way 49 D2
ton Rd 50 B2
usta Pl 51 C1
nue Rd 48 B3
cet Clo 50 B3
lay Rd 50 B1
ack Rd 51 C2
ow Rise 50 A2
on Dri 49 D1
St 51 C1
rd Rd 49 C1
cliff Rd 50 B2
don Clo 49 D1
ch Ct 49 C3
ch View Rd 50 A2
chdown Way 49 C2
ulieu 48 A3
umont Av 48 B3
ord Rd 50 B1
eld Clo 50 B2
eld Park Av 50 B2
eld Park Dri 50 B2
rave 48 A3
rave Cotts 48 B3
Vue Rd 51 C2
mont St 51 C2
dere 51 C1
Nevis Rd 50 B2
ville Rd 50 A1
erley Rd 49 C1
leaves Rd 51 C2
h Way 51 C2
heim Rd 48 B1
ays Dri 50 A3
yn Cres 50 B3
d St 51 C1
king La 49 D2
ton Clo 50 B2
leaze 49 D2
kendown Av 49 C2
ford Rd 50 B2
r Clo 48 A3
bane Rd 49 C1
dlands Rd 48 B1
dmeadow Rd 50 B3
ghton Cres 50 B3
wnlow St 51 C1
el Dri 49 D1
nts Rd 50 A2
Rd 50 B1
mouth Av 49 C2
on Clo 50 B2
Buxton Rd 50 B2
Caledonian Clo 48 B3
Cambridge Rd 50 A1
Camp Rd 50 A3
Canberra Cres 49 C1
Canberra Rd 49 C1
Canterbury Clo 50 A1
Carisbrooke 48 A3
Carlton Rd North 48 B3
Carlton Rd South 48 B3
Caroline Pl 51 C1
Carrington Clo 50 B2
Cassiobury Rd 48 B3
Castle Hill Rd 50 A3
Castlemaine Rd 49 C1
Cedar Dri 49 D1
Chafeys Av 48 A3
Chalbury Clo 49 D1
Chamberlaine Rd 50 A2
Chapel Hay St 51 C2
Charles St 51 C1
Chartwell 48 A3
Chelmsford St 51 C1
Chelwood Gate 50 A1
Cherry Way 49 D2
Chesil Vw 50 A3
Chickerell Rd 50 A1
Churchill Clo 50 A2
Churchward Av 49 D1
Clarence Rd 50 A2
Clarendon Av 48 B1
Clarke Clo 48 A3
Clearmount Rd 50 B3
Cleveland Av 48 B2
Cleves Clo 50 B3
*Clifton Pl,
Gloucester Mews 51 C1
Clive Ter 50 B1
Cobham Dri 50 A1
Cockles La 50 A2
Colchester Way 50 A1
Collett Clo 49 D1
Collins La 50 A3
Comet Clo 50 A2
Commercial Rd 51 C1
Concorde Clo 50 A2
Conifer Way 48 A3
Coniston Cres 48 B2
Connaught Rd 50 B2
Coombe Av 48 B3
Coombe Valley Rd 49 D1
Corfe Rd 48 A2
Cornwall Clo 50 B1
Coronation Cres 48 B2
Coronation Rd 48 B2
Corporation Rd 50 B1
Corporation Yd 51 C1
Court Rd 48 B1
Courtauld Dri 50 B2
*Cove Pl, Cove Rd 51 C2
Cove Rd 51 C2
*Cove St, Cove Rd 51 C2
Coveway 49 D2
Cranford Av 48 B3
Crescent St 51 C1
Cromwell Rd 50 B1
Cross Rd 50 B1
Culliford Way 49 C1
Cumberland Dri 50 A1
Cunningham Clo 50 A2
*Custom House Quay,
Maiden St 51 C2
Dale Av 48 B3
Dawlish Cres 50 B3
Deansleigh 49 D1
Dennis Rd 50 B1
Derby St 51 C1
Derwent Rd 50 B3
Devon Rd 50 B1
Doncaster Rd 50 B3
Dorchester Rd 48 B1
Dorset Clo 50 B1
Dorset Ter 51 C2
Dover Rd 50 B3
Down Clo 50 B3
Down Rd 50 B2
Dumbarton Rd 50 B3
Dundee Rd 50 B3
Eadon Clo 49 D2
East St 51 C2
East Wyld Rd 50 B1
Eastdown Av 49 C2
Eastdown Gdns 49 C2
Ebor Rd 50 A2
Elizabeth Way 50 A1
Elm Clo 49 D2
Emerson Rd 50 B2
Emmadale Rd 50 B1
Enkworth Rd 49 D2
Esplanade 51 C1
Essex Rd 51 C1
Everest Rd 50 B2
Ewell Manor Gdns 51 C2
Fairclose 50 B2
Faircross Av 50 B2
Fairview Rd 50 B3
Farm Clo 48 A3
Faversham 48 A3
Ferndale Rd 48 B3
Fernhill Av 48 B3
Field Barn Dri 48 A3
Fleet Ct 50 A1
Fleetview Rd 50 A3
Forehill Clo 49 D1
Fossett Way 50 A2
Franchise St 51 C2
Francis Rd 50 B2
Franklyn Rd 50 B1
Fraser Av 50 A2
Freemantle Rd 50 A2
Gallwey Rd 50 B3
Garibaldi Row 51 C2
Geelong Clo 49 C1
Gladstone Clo 49 C1
Glebe Clo 50 B2
Glen Av 50 C2
Glendinning Av 48 B3
Glenmore Rd 50 B1
Gloucester Clo 50 A1
Gloucester Mews 51 C1
Gloucester Row 51 C1
Gloucester St 51 C1
Goldcroft Av 51 C1
Goldcroft Rd 48 A3
Gordon Cres 50 A1
Gordon Row 51 C2
Grafton Av 48 A2
Granby Clo 50 A1
Granville Rd 51 C1
Grasmere Clo 48 B2
Grasmere Rd 48 B2
Grays 48 A3
Great George St 51 C1
Green La 50 B2
Greenhill 49 C1
Greenway Clo 48 B2
Greenway Rd 48 B1
*Grosvenor Pl,
Alexandra Gdns 51 C2
Grosvenor Rd 48 B3
*Grosvenors La, East St 51 C2
Grove Av 48 B3
Grove Ter 50 B1
Gypsy La 50 B2
Hamilton Clo 49 C1
Hammond Av 48 A3
Hampshire Rd 50 A1
Hanover Rd 48 B3
Harbour Hill 48 A1
Harbour R/about 51 C2
Hardwick St 51 C1
Hardy Av 50 B2
Hawkesworth Clo 49 D1
Hawthorn Clo 48 A3
Haymoor Clo 49 C2
Haywards Av 48 B2
Hazel Dri 49 D1
Hazeldown Av 49 C2
Heathwood Rd 50 B1
Helen La 51 C2
Herbert Pl 51 C2
Hereford Cres 50 B1
Hereford Rd 50 B1
Hetherly Rd 48 B2
High Down 49 C2
High St 50 A2
High St West 51 C2
High Vw 50 B2
Highland Rd 50 B1
Hill La 51 C2
Hillbourne Clo 50 B3
Hillbourne Rd 50 B3
Hillcrest Rd 50 B3
Holland Rd 51 C1
Holly Rd 50 B1
Hollyrood Ter 51 C1
Hope Sq 51 C2
Hope St 51 C2
Hornbeam Clo 48 A3
Horsford St 51 C2
Howard Clo 50 B3
Icen Rd 48 B2
Ilchester Rd 51 C1
James St 51 C2
Jasmine Way 50 A2
John St 51 C2
Johns Ct 51 C1
Jubilee Clo 51 C1
Kayes Clo 50 B3
Kellaway Ter 51 C1
Kempston Rd 51 C2
Kenilworth 48 A3
Kenmoor Clo 49 C2
Kent Clo 50 A1
Kimberley Clo 49 C1
Kimmeridge Clo 48 A2
King St 51 C1
Kingfisher Clo 50 B3
Kings R/about 51 C1
Kings Rd 48 B2
Kingsbere Rd 49 D2
Kirtleton Av 48 B3
Kitchener Rd 50 B1
Knightsdale Rd 50 B1
Knoll Rise 49 C1
Laburnum Clo 48 A2
Lakeside Gdns 48 B2
Lancaster Rd 48 B1
Lanehouse Rocks Rd 50 A1
Langton Av 50 B3
Lansdown Sq 51 C2
Lea Rd 50 A2
Leamington Rd 50 A1
Leeds Cres 50 A1
Lennox St 51 C1
Lessingham Av 50 A3
Lichfield Rd 50 A1
Lincoln Rd 50 A1
Lindens Clo 48 B3
Links Rd 50 B1
Littlemoor Rd 49 C1
Littleview Rd 50 A2
Liverpool Rd 50 A2
Lodge Way 50 B2
Lodmoor Av 48 B2
Lomond Dri 50 B2
Longcroft Rd 50 B1
Longfield Rd 51 C2
Look Out 51 C2
Lorton La 48 B1
Louviers Rd 49 C1
Love La 51 C2
Lower Bond St 51 C1
Lower St Albans St 51 C1
Lower St Edmunds St 51 C2
Ludlow Rd 50 A1
Lydwell Clo 50 B2
Lynch La 50 A1
Lynch Rd 50 A1
Lyndale Rd 50 B3
Lyndhurst Rd 48 B3
Lynmoor Rd 49 C1
Maiden St 51 C2
Malvern Ter 50 B1
Mandeville Clo 50 A2
Mandeville Rd 50 A2
Manor Rd 48 B2
Marina Gdns 50 B2
Market St 51 C2
Markham Av 50 B2
Marlborough Av 50 B3
Marlow Rd 51 C2
Marquis Clo 50 A1
Marsh Rd 51 C2
Martleaves Clo 50 B2
Maunsell Av 49 D1
Maycroft Rd 51 C2
Mayfield Clo 48 A3
Mead Rd 48 A3
Medway Dri 49 D1
Melbourne St 50 B1
Melbury Rd 51 C1
Melcombe Av 49 C1
Melstock Av 49 D2
Merley Rd 50 B3
Milton Clo 48 B3
Milton Cres 48 B3
Milton Rd 51 C1
Milton Ter 48 B3
*Mitchell St, East St 51 C2
Monmouth Rd 48 B2
Moorcombe Dri 49 D1
Moordown Av 49 C2
Mount Pleasant 48 B2
Mount Pleasant Av 48 B2
Mount St 51 C2
Mountbatten Clo 50 A2
Mulberry Ter 51 C1
Neterton Rd 51 C2
New Clo 50 A3
New Close Gdns 51 C2
New Rd 51 C2
Newberry Gdns 51 C2
Newberry Rd 51 C2

Newstead Rd	51 C1
Newtons Rd	51 C2
Nicholas St	51 C1
Norfolk Rd	50 B1
North Quay	51 C2
North Rd	50 A2
Nothe Parade	51 C2
Nothe Walk	51 D3
Nottington Ct	48 A1
Nottington La	48 A1
Nutgrove Av	50 A2
Oak Way	49 C2
Oakbury Dri	49 D2
Oakley Pl	51 C2
Old Castle Rd	50 B3
Old Parish La	50 B1
Orchard Dri	49 D1
Orion Rd	51 C2
Osprey Rd	50 B3
Overbury Clo	50 A1
Overcombe Dri	49 D2
Overlands Rd	50 A2
Park Ct	49 C1
Park La	48 B3
Park Mead Rd	50 B3
Park St	51 C1
Penny St	51 C1
Perth St	50 B1
Pirates La	50 A3
Poplar Clo	48 A3
Portland Cres	50 B1
Portland Rd	50 B2
Portwey Clo	51 C2
Preston Rd	49 C1
Pretoria Ter	50 B2
Prince of Wales Rd	50 B2
Princess Dri	48 B3
Prospect Pl	51 C2
Putton La	50 A1
Queen St	51 C1
Queens Rd	48 B2
Queensland Rd	50 B1
Quibo La	50 B1
Radipole Ct	48 B3
Radipole La	50 B1
Radipole Park Dri	51 C1
Radipole Ter	48 B3
Ranelagh Rd	51 C1
Raymond Rd	50 A2
Rectory Way	50 B2
Redcliff Vw	51 C2
Reed View Clo	48 A3
Rhose Wood Dri	49 D1
Rochester Cl	50 B1
Rockhampton Clo	49 C1
Rodwell Av	51 C2
Rodwell Rd	51 C2
Rodwell St	51 C2
Roman Clo	48 B2
Roman Rd	48 B2
Rosecroft Rd	50 A2
Roundham Gdns	50 B2
Roundhayes Clo	50 B1
Rowan Clo	48 A3
Rowland Ct	49 C1
Royal Cres	51 C1
Royal Ter	51 C1
Russell Av	50 B2
Rutland Rd	50 B1
Ryemead La	50 A3
Rylands La	50 B2
St Andrews Av	48 B2
St Annes Rd	50 B3
St Davids Rd	50 B3
St Georges Av	48 B3
St Helens Rd	50 A1
St Leonards Rd	51 C2
St Martins Rd	50 B3
St Marys St	51 C2
St Patricks Av	50 A2
St Thomas St	51 C2
Salisbury Rd	51 C1
Sanbourne Rd	49 D1
Sandpiper Way	50 B3
School St	51 C1
Seamoor Clo	49 C2
Sedgefield Clo	50 B1
Shears Rd	48 B2
Shirecroft Rd	50 B1
Short Rd	50 B1
Shrubbery La	50 A2
Somerset Rd	50 B1
South Par	51 C2
South Rd	50 A3
Southcroft Rd	50 A2
Southdown Av	49 C2
Southdown Rd	50 B3
Southfield Av	48 B3
Southill Gardens Dri	48 A3
Southlands Rd	50 B3
Southview Rd	50 B1
Spa Av	48 B2
Spa Rd	48 A2
Spring Av	51 C2
Spring Gdns	51 C2
Spring La	51 C2
Spring Rd	51 C2
Stainforth Clo	50 B1
Stanier Rd	49 D1
Stanley St	51 C1
Stavordale Rd	51 C1
Steeple Clo	48 B2
Stirling Rd	48 B2
Stoborough Clo	48 B2
Stoke Rd	50 B3
Studland Way	48 A2
Sunnyside Rd	50 B3
Sussex Rd	50 B1
Sutcliffe Av	48 A2
Sycamore Rd	48 A3
Sydney St	50 B1
Teeling Rd	48 B2
Tennyson Rd	50 B2
The Cherries	48 B2
The Rise	48 A3
The Spinney	48 B1
The Square	50 A2
Tollerdown Rd	50 A1
Trinity Rd	51 C2
Trinity St	51 C2
Trinity Ter	51 C2
*Turton St. Gloucester Mews	51 C1
Tyneham Clo	48 A2
Ullswater Cres	48 A2
Underbarn Wk	51 C3
Upway St	51 C1
Vanguard Av	50 A2
Verne Clo	51 C2
Verne Rd	51 C2
Verne Way	51 C2
Victoria Rd	50 B3
Victoria St	51 C1
Victoria Ter	51 C1
Viscount Rd	50 A2
Vulcan Clo	50 A2
Wainwright Clo	49 D1
Walker Cres	50 B3
Walpole St	51 C1
Wardcliffe Rd	50 B1
Warren Clo	50 A1
Waverley Rd	48 B3
Wellington Ct	51 C2
Wentworth Clo	49 C1
Wesley St	51 C1
Wessex Rd	50 B1
West Bay Cres	50 A3
West St	51 C2
Westbourne Rd	48 B3
Westdowne Clo	50 B1
Westerhall Rd	49 C1
Westham R./about	51 C2
Westham Rd	51 C1
Westhaven	50 B1
Westhill Clo	50 A3
Westhill Rd	50 A3
Weston Rd	51 C2
Westwey Rd	51 C2
Weymouth Bay Av	48 B3
White Cross Dri	50 B2
Williams Av	50 B3
Willow Cres	49 D1
Wilton Dri	50 B2
Wiltshire Av	50 B1
Winchester Clo	50 A1
Windermere Cres	48 B2
Wingreen	49 D1
Winton Clo	48 A3
*Woodperton St, Westham Rd	51 C1
Wyke Oliver Clo	49 D1
Wyke Oliver Rd	49 D1
Wyke Rd	50 B2

WIMBORNE MINSTER

Allen Ct	53 A2
Allen Rd	53 B3
Allenview Rd	53 A2
Ashdene	53 B2
Avenue Rd	53 B3
Barnes Cres	53 B3
Beaucroft La	53 B2
Beaucroft Rd	53 B2
Beaufort Dri	53 B2
Birchdale Rd	53 B2
Blind La	53 A2
Boundary Dri	53 B1
Bourne Court	53 B2
Bradbury Vw	53 B2
Brook Rd	53 B3
Burts Hill	53 B1
Byron Rd	53 B2
Cemetery Rd	53 A2
Chapel La	53 A2
Charles Keightly Clo	53 B3
Chaucer Clo	53 A2
Chene Rd	53 B2
Cheriton Way	53 B2
Chestnut Clo	53 B2
Church St	53 A2
Churchill Rd	53 B3
Cobbs Rd	53 B1
Cooks Row	53 A2
Coppercourt Lease	53 B3
Cornmarket	53 A2
Courtenay Dri	53 B2
Cowgrove Rd	53 A2
Cranbourne Rd	53 A1
Cranfield Av	53 B3
Crescent Rd	53 B3
Cromwell Rd	53 B3
Crown Mead	53 A2
Culverhayes Rd	53 A2
Cuthburga Rd	53 A2
Cuthbury Clo	53 A2
Cuthbury Gdns	53 A2
Days Ct	53 B3
Deans Court La	53 A2
Deans Gro	53 B1
Derwent Water Rd	53 B3
Dogdean	53 B1
East Borough	53 A2
East St	53 A2
Eden Gro	53 B3
Elizabeth Rd	53 A2
Ethelbert Rd	53 B3
Fairfield Rd	53 B2
Furzehill	53 A1
Giddylake	53 B2
Glendale Clo	53 B2
Gordon Rd	53 B3
Green Close La	53 B2
Greenhill Clo	53 B1
Greenhill La	53 B2
Greenhill Rd	53 B2
Greenways Rise	53 A2
Grenville Rd	53 B3
Grove Rd	53 B3
Gullivers Ct	53 A2
Hanham Rd	53 A2
Hardy Cres	53 B3
High St	53 A2
Highland Rd	53 B2
Highland View Clo	53 B2
Hornbeam Clo	53 B2
Ingram Walk	53 B3
Julians Rd	53 A2
King St	53 A2
Knobcrook Rd	53 A2
Lacy Clo	53 B2
Lacy Dri	53 B2
Legg La	53 B2
Leigh Gdns	53 B3
Leigh Rd	53 B2
Lewens La	53 B2
Livingstone Rd	53 B3
Long La	53 B1
Lower Ct	53 B3
Marlborough Pl	53 B2
Melverley Gdns	53 B2
Merley Ways	53 B3
Mill La	53 A2
Mill Stream Clo	53 A2
Milton Rd	53 A2
Minster Vw	53 B2
New Borough Rd	53 B3
Oakdale	53 B2
Oakley Hill	53 B3
Oakley Rd	53 B3
Old Highway Mews	53 A2
Old Rd	53 A2
Onslow Gdns	53 B2
Osborne Rd	53 B3
Park La	53 A2
Parkwood Rd	53 B2
Pine Tree Clo	53 B2
Poole Rd	53 B3
Poplar Clo	53 A2
Priors Walk	53 A2
Quince La	53 B2
Redcotts La	5
Redcotts Rd	5
Retreat Rd	5
Richmond Rd	5
River Clo	5
Rowlands Hill	5
Royston Dri	5
School La	5
Sheppards Field	5
Shakespeare Rd	5
Smugglers La	5
St Catherines	5
St Johns Hill	5
St Margarets Clo	5
St Margarets Hill	5
Station Rd	5
Station Ter	5
Stone La	5
Tapper Ct	5
Tennyson Rd	5
The Square	5
Tower La	5
Trumpeters Ct	5
Ullswater Rd	5
Ventor Pl	5
Victoria Pl	5
Victoria Rd	5
Walford Clo	5
Welland Rd	5
Wesley Rd	5
Wesley Rd	5
West Borough	5
West Row	5
West St	5
Westfield	5
Whitehouse Rd	5
Whiteways	5
Willett Rd	5
Willow Clo	5
Wimborne By-Pass	5
Wimborne Rd	5
Wimborne Rd	5
Yew Tree Clo	5

WOOL

Baileys Dri	54
Bindon La	54
Bindon Way	54
Breachfield	54
Burton La	54
Chain Pit La	54
Church La	54
Colliers La	54
Cottage Clo	54
Dorchester Rd	54
Duck St	54
East Burton Rd	54
Fairfields	54
Folly La	54
Frome Av	54
*Giddy Grn	54
Giddy Green Rd	54
High St	54
High Street Clo	54
Hillside Rd	54
Hyde Rd	54
Hyde Way	54
Jeremy Clo	54
Knowle Hill	54
Knowlewood Knap	54
Lampton Clo	54
Linclieth Rd	54
Lower Hillside Rd	54
Lulworth Rd	54
Meadow La	54
Moreton Rd	54
New Buildings Rd	54
New Rd	54
Oakdene Rd	54
Quarr Hill	54
Spring St	54
Station Rd	54
Sydenham Cres	54
The Cross	54
The Square	54
Vicarage Clo	54
Wareham Rd	54